In the Light of
MEDITATION

In the Light of
MEDITATION

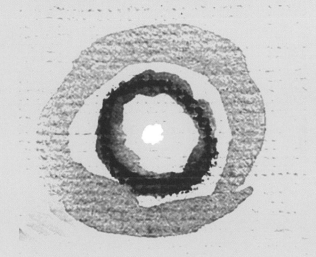

A Guide to Meditation
and Spiritual Development

Mike George

BRAHMA KUMARIS
WORLD SPIRITUAL UNIVERSITY

BOOKS
Winchester, UK • New York, USA

Copyright © 2004 O Books
O Books is an imprint of John Hunt Publishing Ltd.,
Deershot Lodge, Park Lane, Ropley, Hants, SO24 0BE, UK
office@johnhunt-publishing.com
www.O-books.net

Distribution in;
UK
Orca Book Services, orders@orcabookservices.co.uk
Tel: 01202 665432 Fax: 01202 666219 Int. code (44)

USA and Canada
NBN, custserv@nbnbooks.com
Tel: 1 800 462 6420 Fax: 1 800 338 4550

Australia
Brumby Books, sales@brumbybooks.com
Tel: 61 3 9761 5535 Fax: 61 3 9761 7095

New Zealand
Peaceful Living, books@peaceful-living.co.nz
Tel: 64 7 57 18105 Fax: 64 7 57 18513

Singapore
STP, davidbuckland@tlp.com.sg
Tel: 65 6276 Fax: 65 6276 7119

South Africa
Alternative Books, altbook@global.co.za
Tel: 27 011 792 7730 Fax: 27 011 972 7787

Text: © 2004 Brahma Kumaris Information Services Ltd.
65 Pound Lane, London NW10 2HH

Reprinted 2005, 2007

Designed by Krave Ltd., London, UK

ISBN 1 903816 61 0

A CIP catalogue record for this book is available from the British Library.

Printed by Tien Wah Press Ltd., Singapore

This book is dedicated

*to those who seek the deepest peace, the greatest love
and the truest happiness in life*

*to those for whom all is not what it appears to be
but who cannot quite see behind appearances!*

*to those who simply seek to know
what is truth and what is illusion*

*to those who know they are not being true to themselves
and are moved to live with greater authenticity and integrity*

*to those who are aware that this world is on the edge of a dramatic
and profound shift, and sense they have a significant role to play*

*to those who know a higher power is now at work in the world
and hear the subtle call of that power to be present and available*

*to those who simply wish to know exactly
who they are and why on earth they are here*

Contents

Preface

The Foundation Course in Meditation

Welcome to the Foundation Course in Raja Yoga Meditation. The purpose of this book is to offer you an introduction to the art and practice of meditation while laying down the foundations for ongoing spiritual development. This particular method of meditation and approach to spiritual development has been the core teaching of the Brahma Kumaris World Spiritual University for over sixty years and is now practised daily by over four hundred and fifty thousand people in eighty-six countries.

Meditation is more an experience than something that you do, more a process than an achievement, more an ongoing inner journey than a destination. Take your time, be patient with yourself and always be ready to go back to basics, to Lesson One, the true identity of the self, which is the foundation of everything.

About the
Brahma Kumaris
World Spiritual University

The Brahma Kumaris World Spiritual University is an international educational organisation with more than five thousand centres in over eighty countries. The University offers a variety of courses, workshops and seminars aimed at helping individuals to develop their full spiritual, intellectual and mental capacities.

For over sixty years, the main course and foundation of the University's teaching has been this particular course in Raja Yoga Meditation. The spiritual insights and understanding contained within the course were consolidated by the founder of the University, Brahma Baba, between 1937 and 1969. He dedicated the final third of his life to the spiritual service of others. During this time, while refusing to see himself as a guru, he was seen as an instrument to crystallise in words and actions the basic universal truths which both transcend and unite all other religious and moral philosophies. Perhaps his greatest legacy was to show how those truths could be applied and integrated into a contemporary way of life and make a positive difference to human relationships.

The University exists to serve the global community and makes no charge for any of the courses or events that it conducts. It is funded by voluntary contributions.

How to use this book

Each lesson comprises specific insights into Raja Yoga Meditation, with practical meditation exercises to complement and to help your understanding of the method and the underlying teachings. Where appropriate, a glossary of terms is footnoted. It is recommended that you move slowly through each lesson, digesting the information, giving due time to the exercises and allowing yourself to begin to experience the benefits of each in your life. At the end of each lesson there is a journal with exercises to help you deepen your understanding through personal reflection and monitor your own progress. Here are a few pointers to aid your study:

- It is advisable to read this book in a different way from other books. We suggest that you take your time and actually study what you are reading. You may want to go through a lesson quickly at first, just to get the general idea of what is being taught. You will then need to go back and read through, step by step, doing the exercises carefully. Then, when you are ready, put whatever you think you have learnt into practice. Each chapter requires deep consideration and meditation practice to be fully absorbed and assimilated.

- One lesson per week is recommended with daily reading of that lesson.

- When you get time during the day, review and reflect on one or two points from the lesson you are working with during that week.

- Plan time for your meditation practice at least twice a day (early morning and before you sleep are recommended times).

- We recommend that you listen to the recorded meditations on the accompanying CD.

When you reach the end of each lesson you will find:

- Frequently Asked Questions and answers which may address some of the questions you have yourself.

- Journal exercises to enhance and deepen your understanding of that lesson.

- A personal experience from someone who has benefited from the practice of Raja Yoga Meditation.

Any Questions?

If you are learning Raja Yoga Meditation for the first time and you would like some assistance, an experienced meditator will be happy to send you a personal response to your questions. This will give you the opportunity to clarify any aspect of both the theory and method that comprise this course.

Please send your email to **meditation@bkpublications.com**

Please state your question, country and first language.

Introduction

Why Raja Yoga Meditation?
What you can gain from this course

It is not by accident that the practice of meditation lies at the heart of almost all the great spiritual traditions and paths of wisdom. Meditation has always been the most effective way to explore and understand the mystery and the beauty of our spirit, empower our true self, and discern the significance and purpose of our life. It has also been the first and most important stepping stone to restoring our personal relationship with the Divine.

People learn to meditate for a variety of reasons. For many it is simply a desire for inner peace, for others it is part of their quest for truth and understanding, and for some it is the hope of discovering the holy grail of happiness. Meditation can satisfy each of these desires. However, a common misconception is that meditation can be learned simply by listening to a lecture or reading about it. While we may intellectually understand the process and benefits of meditation, these will be of little value until there is practice and direct experience on a daily basis. This meditation course is designed to facilitate such an experience. It is therefore recommended that you give a minimum of one week to each lesson, before moving on to the next.

The Mental and Physical Benefits of Meditation

Meditation helps us to experience the unlimited nature of our minds, which is only possible when we are free of uncontrolled mental chatter. In the process of freeing ourselves from inner noise, we come to understand more deeply the relationship between our conscious and subconscious mind. It becomes easier to control our emotions, and our intuitive capacity is enhanced. The principle benefits are improved levels of contentment, concentration, creativity and communication. These, in turn, are the foundations of both our own personal well-being and our harmonious relationships with others.

A recurring theme during the course is the importance of recognising our true spiritual identity, and the understanding that we are innately peaceful and positive individuals, regardless of how we feel today. Anger, fear and depression are unnatural and learned. Meditation helps us to see the roots of all negative thoughts and feelings, unlearn and heal their causes, and rediscover our inner peace so that *contentment* becomes possible in every situation.

Surrounded by a highly-charged, constantly-changing world, we find it hard to maintain our attention on any one thing for any length of time. Stress and tiredness are our modern malaise. Meditation is a gentle retraining of our minds in the art of *concentration*, giving ourselves the chance to look more deeply into the still waters of our own consciousness, while staying focused on the outer task at hand. Our ability to be creative begins on the canvas of our own minds. Here is where we paint the magnificent panorama of our own life, with the brushstrokes and colours of our own thoughts and feelings. Meditation helps us to stand back from the canvas and consciously choose what we want to be, do and achieve. Any limitations in our

creative capacity are self-imposed. Meditation can melt those inner barriers and blocks that we have erected within ourselves, allowing our full potential to flourish.

The practical application and benefits of meditation will eventually show up in our interpersonal relationships. As our inner peace and positivity are restored by regular practice, meditation helps us to shape the energy we share with others, and we find it easier to resolve conflict, remain open, *communicate* honestly with others and ultimately be of help to others through the quality of the company we are able to give.

There are also many physical benefits which can result from the sustained practice of meditation. It is now well documented and widely recognised that meditation has a deeply relaxing and calming effect on the nervous system, balancing physical energies, allowing the body to function more effectively while improving its ability to heal itself. This can result in reduced blood pressure, an increase in vitality, better sleep patterns and greater pain control.

The Spiritual Benefits

As meditation improves our awareness of both mind and body, we learn to listen to their signals and more easily recognise and meet their needs. One of the unique features of this particular course is both the understanding of the true nature of spirit and the direct spiritual experience it may give you. In this context, spirituality should not be confused with religious belief. The core purpose of the spiritual knowledge within this course is to help you understand and experience yourself as you really are, a spiritual being, and to rediscover your innate spiritual qualities – peace, love, happiness and power – not as intellectual ideas but as actual experience.

Raja Yoga has two meanings: 'Sovereign Yoga', the yoga through which I become the sovereign, the master of myself; and the 'Supreme Union', or 'Union with the Supreme'. This second aspect of Raja Yoga involves rediscovering and developing a personal relationship with the Supreme, the Source of perfection, God.

It is worth emphasising that Raja Yoga is not a religious path, but more a universal approach to spiritual awakening and development. It does not preclude or deny any religious beliefs or practices. In fact, thousands of students who attend Brahma Kumaris Raja Yoga Meditation Centres worldwide have found that both the understanding and practice of Raja Yoga Meditation have positively enhanced their own religious understanding and practice.

Whether you want to learn how to relax, need to be more concentrated and creative, or are searching deeply for spiritual enlightenment, this particular course can satisfy each of those needs.

What is Meditation?

An introduction to the practice of meditation

For many people, meditation is perceived as something only for monks on mountains in the East. For others, it is a throwback to the swinging sixties era of hippy 'love and peace', accompanied by a reckless culture of 'anything goes'. The truth, however, is that the word meditation is derived from the Latin mederi, meaning 'to heal'. Meditation can certainly be considered as a healing process – spiritual, mental and emotional – with proven benefits to physical well-being. If we are wise enough to acknowledge our own negative thoughts and emotions (and for many of us these can be dominant aspects of our personality), and if we can acknowledge that stress is not a normal part of a fulfilling life, then we can reap many rewards from the regular practice of meditation and the gentle healing process which meditation provides.

One of the simplest definitions of meditation is 'the correct use of the mind'. The initial aim of meditation is not to deny our thoughts, but to become aware of our mind, gain mastery over our mental activity and generate the highest quality of thoughts. In time, with practice, we will be able to slow down our thoughts and enter the inner space within our own consciousness, where there is no conscious thought, only silence. Initially, however, this need not be our aim. We are more accustomed to thinking fast and often frenetic thoughts. Trying to stop thinking would be like slamming on the brakes of a car while doing 80 mph. We need to be patient with ourselves and give ourselves the time and space to slow down and find our natural inner rhythm.

There are many approaches to meditation and methods of meditative practice available today. Each philosophy or style recognises the power and influence of the mind and many methods have the aim of mental mastery. Most employ contemplation and concentration exercises, often using objects such as flowers or candles, or perhaps sounds which move from a continuous tone into silence. Other techniques involve the repetition of a mantra as the mental focus. While most approaches recommend that the body is still, some include meditation on the move and mindful walking. Raja Yoga Meditation does not involve the use of external objects, physical postures or mantras. Rather, the two main aims are to restore the direct experience and awareness of the self as spirit, and to recreate the subtle link with the Source of spirit. Through a gentle process of self-realisation and a reconnection with the Supreme, both the enlightenment and the transformation of the self take place[1].

If we took time to explore the real root causes of all forms of stress, we would find that both lazy and distorted thinking lie behind the various emotions that we find stressful. In most developed cultures, no-one tells us that we are each responsible for our own thoughts and feelings. We miss learning the lesson of inner self-responsibility which reminds us that we create our own stress in life by the way we perceive and respond to others and the world. Instead we are taught that others are responsible for what we think and feel. We then project our stress onto others under the illusion that 'they' are responsible for our suffering. No-one teaches us 'how' to think. We are told only 'what' to think in terms of information, but not how to shape our own thoughts and feelings, nor how to draw on the innate wisdom and core values which can be found within the consciousness of every human being.[2]

At the heart of this course, there is an opportunity to teach yourself to think positive and powerful thoughts; thoughts which are connected to truth, beneficial to your own well-being and that bring a positive energy to those around you; thoughts which are relevant to the context in which you find yourself and thoughts which use all your energies in an economical way; thoughts which ensure that the outcome of any response you may create does not result in stressful emotions. When no-one teaches us in our formal education systems that any mental or emotional discomfort comes from within our own consciousness, it ensures that we fail to realise that any negative state of being is unnatural and a sign that our consciousness is 'out of shape'. Meditation allows us to return our consciousness to its true, natural and original shape. This happens through a gradual increase in self-awareness, an awakening to who we really are and the rediscovery of our natural inner resources of peace, power and love.

Most of us spend a large part of our life being over aware of everyone and everything around us. This can easily have the effect of draining our energy without our realising it. Meditation is the art of cultivating self-awareness so we can become more skilful at using

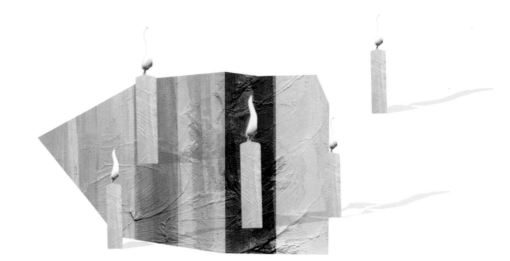

our energy – mental, emotional and physical – in ways which
increase our inner resources, not deplete them. In many ways
meditation is simply the art of self-awareness.

Meditation can also be seen as an exploration of truth, the truth of
who and what you really are. In that sense, you are like a scientist in
a laboratory. The laboratory is your own consciousness – only you
have access to the laboratory, and all your experiments can be top
secret if you wish! This course is an invitation to enter the
laboratory of your consciousness where you can quietly explore,
experiment and experience what is true or not true for you. The only
caution is that if an insight or exercise does not appear to be having
the expected effect, don't be too hasty and throw the baby out with
the bath water. Practice, persistence and patience were the
prerequisite qualities when we learned to ride our first bike. The
same applies with the inner exercise which meditation allows you to
do. Practice and patience make perfect.

As you progress in your meditation practice, becoming more self-
aware and experiencing your own inner peace, you will also begin to
see the unfolding of a factual story. It is a non-fictional narrative
that makes Raja Yoga quite distinct from all other approaches to

meditation and spiritual understanding, lifting it away from being just another method of mental relaxation and into a deeper spiritual territory. The combination of the narrative which is revealed within this course and the practice of meditation sheds light on those age-old questions concerning the purpose, meaning and significance of both our individual and collective lives.   That narrative comes later. First, it is necessary to understand and assimilate the essential insights into the self, and then begin the practice of meditation as the method to know and understand the self directly.

While resolving the essential questions of 'Who am I, where am I, why am I here, where do I come from and where am I going?', there is a good chance that you will gain many new insights into your own spiritual journey. However, your meditation practice will likely create further spiritual questions. This is a good sign, for in truth, in all things truly spiritual, the questions are often more important than the answers. If and when questions do come, take a moment to clarify each question and then let it go. Release it. Never struggle to find answers. In fact, never struggle. You'll be surprised how quickly your subconscious will supply you with the insight and guidance appropriate to your needs. All that you need to know, you already know, it's just that you are not aware of it. Sometimes when attempting to complete a crossword puzzle you might mull over clues before giving up and going on to another question. Later in the day, while carrying out another activity, the word you were searching for will suddenly jump into your mind. You were not consciously looking for the answer, but the mind continued to do its own research on another level. Meditation gently opens the treasure chest of your subconscious, giving you access to your own heart, the core of your consciousness, where your own wisdom lies in its completeness. It will speak to you directly, perhaps not at the most convenient times, probably when you are least distracted and able to recognise its call. One of its voices is called intuition. Our intuition loves meditation.

We are all now aware of the 'psychosomatic effect', where many physical diseases are recognised, directly and indirectly, to have their roots in mental dis-ease (negative thinking). In its most basic practice, meditation is a way of ensuring that our mind creates only relaxed, calm, peaceful and positive thoughts. This does not mean avoiding the challenges of modern life, which are not always peaceful and positive. However, it does mean that we can learn to eliminate any negative, disturbing thoughts and restore a positive inner mental environment, regardless of outer events and circumstances. This is then the basis for building self-control, self-esteem and self-respect, which provide the foundation for self-confidence and the appropriate assertiveness in our relationships. As we saw earlier the purpose of meditation is not to stop our thoughts, that would be unnatural at this stage, but to generate a positive flow of right thought, positive thought, based on an accurate understanding of 'the self'.

 The first step in learning to meditate is to relax both your body and your mind, and to free them from any distractions. When we make the distinction between mind and matter, body and soul, human and being, form and consciousness, we are intuitively making a distinction between two kinds of energy – physical (matter) and non-physical (spirit). Our bodies are made of the five elements of matter, which combine to make our physical forms both visible and tangible. Our minds are non-physical energy, which produces intangible, invisible thoughts, feelings and attitudes. To understand this more clearly, consider the case of electricity: you know it exists because you can see the result in the form of an electric light, but you cannot see the actual electricity. In the same way the mind cannot be seen but the energy which comes through it directs the movement of the body.

The right relationship between mind and body is where the mind is the captain and the body is the ship, following the captain's orders. Today, however, it is often the other way around. We are ruled by our physical senses, and in many of our cultures we are obsessed with physical appearances and physical stimulation. The result is that we have made our peace and happiness dependent on external, physical sources. This can be disastrous because nothing outside is constant and reliable. If we do rely on any external situation or substances for our inner 'feel good factor', then greed, addiction and dependency are not far away, and inner peace and contentment are impossible. In short, our mind is disturbed. Unfortunately, our education and cultural conditioning tend to teach us to reach outwards and not inwards to find love, peace and contentment, whereas almost all the ancient paths of wisdom remind us to turn our attention and awareness inside, where we will find that the peace, contentment and power that we seek have been present all along. Meditation restores our awareness of our innate peace and spiritual power within, reconnecting us with these states of being, allowing us to bring them out into our personality and, through our actions, into the world.

In this first lesson, our aim is simply to restore the right relationship between our mind and our body. When you sit to meditate, choose the quietest place you can find, preferably in a room that you do not use very often. If this isn't possible, sit where the familiar objects around you won't distract your attention. If you can, set this place aside purely for the purpose of meditation. Start with ten or fifteen minutes. This will gradually lengthen with experience. Soft or subdued lighting will help as will some soft background music of your choice. Alternatively, you may play the appropriate part of the tape or CD that complements the lessons in this book.

Relaxing into Meditation

- Sit comfortably in your chosen meditation place...
- Close your eyes and, for a minute or two, allow your body and mind to slow down by remaining still and quiet...
- While keeping your eyes closed, take your attention to your toes...
- Clench them tightly for a moment, then relax them...
- Do this twice more...
- Then consciously relax the muscles in your toes...
- Work progressively, but slowly, up your body tensing and releasing and relaxing your calves, then your thighs, buttocks, stomach, chest, arms, shoulders, back, hands, forearms, jaw, eyes and brow...
- Be aware that your whole body is now relaxed in the chair and that all your attention is focused in the middle of the forehead...
- With your attention solely on your thoughts, let your thoughts float to the surface, then imagine them dissolving ...
- Allow quietness to pervade your mind – as if you were listening to silence...
- If any sensation or thoughts come to distract you, simply let them pass on through your mind...
- Then return your attention to the quietness in your mind...
- Acknowledge your inner relaxation with a quiet thought, "My mind is now calmer, and I feel more peaceful"...
- After a few minutes, bring your awareness back to the room and the here and now.

This relaxation exercise is simple to do, relaxing and energising, and easy to integrate into busy days. All you need are three or four minutes anywhere, any time – except in the car! Note how you were consciously using your mind to relax your body. Once your body is relaxed, it allows you to provide your mind with positive, undivided attention. The more you practise this experience, the easier it becomes. Eventually you won't need to work through your body, muscle by muscle – it will relax almost instantly with just one thought.

In our next meditation, we will focus on the quality or state of inner peace. This is a good beginning, especially if our life is often punctuated by frequent periods of upheaval or stress. There is an important principle that lies behind the success of meditation – where attention goes, energy flows; and where energy flows, things grow. As we 'give' our mental attention to the idea of peace, we water it with the energy of our consciousness; it grows from a thought into a deep feeling and the result is the experience of inner peace – our thoughts and feelings become peace full, and our words and actions then have a peaceful vibration behind them.

Inner peace is not a passive or submissive state. It is a state of inner power and you will soon notice how much more creative you become as you learn to calm your mind consciously and take command of your inner world. Experiment with the thoughts below in your meditation, twice a day for the next week, perhaps exchanging peace for other qualities such as courage, honesty, love, patience, flexibility, or any other quality you would like to grow or strengthen within yourself.

Gentle, but unobtrusive, background music may be played, as this helps to create a relaxed and light atmosphere. Position the text in front of you and read over the following words slowly and silently.

Aim to experience and visualise the words in your mind so that you begin to feel what is being described. Once you have read them once or twice, you will be able to recall them with sufficient accuracy during the day. Alternatively, play the cassette or CD that has been recorded to go with this book.

Meditation 1 – Restoring Inner Peace

I imagine that nothing exists outside this room...
I imagine that the room itself is now empty of any objects...
There is nothing to distract me...
I remove my awareness from my physical body and turn my attention inwards...
I become aware of many thoughts going through my mind...
I become the silent observer of my own thoughts watching each thought come and then move on...
Thoughts come and then they pass like clouds in the sky...
As I witness my thoughts, they begin to slow down...
I focus my attention on the idea of peace...
A wave of peace gently washes over me, removing all restlessness and tension from my mind ...
There is just peace...
In this moment, it is as if ... I ... am ... peace
Peace and quiet and stillness – peace feels so natural...
Like water that is fresh, still and clear, my mind is now calm and clear...
I feel an easiness that is free from all tension...
There is deep contentment within...
I realise this is my most natural state of being...
Having returned to my natural state of peace, I sit for a while, enjoying these feelings of calmness and serenity...

I visualise a situation that I know I will soon face at work or at home
I see how I can maintain my state of inner peace and how it affects
my thoughts and words...
I can feel the power of peace in my actions...
I gently rehearse the scene and begin to see how the power of my
inner peace is reflected back to me by those around me...
With this feeling of total peace, I gently return my thoughts and
awareness to this physical body to this room.

For some people, it is useful to give the specific quality of inner
peace an inner image to contemplate. For example, peace may be a
flat, calm lake. For a meditation on flexibility, perhaps a reed
swaying in the wind will help. The secret is not to get stuck on the
image, but to use it to evoke certain feelings and then to
acknowledge that the theme with which you started your meditation
is now your state of being.

Practise the above for about ten minutes at least twice a day. The
best times are in the morning before the day starts and then once
again in the evening.

Frequently Asked Questions

Q. *It seems that the focus of this course is primarily on the mind and spirit. Isn't care of the physical body important, too?*

A. Yes it is. Our physical body is acknowledged as essential to our life and the art of living. It is our vehicle and our dwelling. An appropriate balance of diet, rest, relaxation and exercise is always recommended. However, during this course you will notice that the main emphasis is on mind and spirit. This does not mean that we do not value or take care of our body. Without a healthy body, we would not be able to express ourselves mentally or spiritually. Unfortunately, though, we have lost the wisdom of balance and for too long we have placed too much emphasis on our physical form, to the detriment of our mental capacity and spiritual awareness. One of the aims of this course is to restore the balance between mind, body and spirit so that we can achieve well-being at every level. So while our body and our physical energy is essential, the focus of this course is on mind and spirit, to help redress the balance.

Q. *I started doing meditation at the same time as a good friend of mine. However, I don't seem to be making as much progress as she is. What am I doing wrong?*

A. The key is to be patient with yourself. Many people try to meditate but find it hard to sit still and quieten the mind. Our journeys to this point are very different and, as a consequence, we all have different personalities. Some take to meditation like a duck to water, but if you have a challenge getting started, be patient with yourself. For others, it can take weeks or sometimes months before they feel they are really beginning to practise and experience the benefits. There is no way to measure how you are progressing apart from your own experience. The main thing is not to expect anything specific. Some people see light, others feel more peaceful and others feel more powerful and in control. Never compare your experience with others. However, it does help if you can meditate with others. In a mutually supportive atmosphere, we make it easier for each other to enter a meditative state.

Q. *You say that we already know all that we need to know so why can't I just listen to my intuition?*

A. That would be ideal but unfortunately most of us are not able to hear the voice of our own wisdom because the noise of our thoughts and feelings drowns it out. As you will see we are all gatherers and assimilators of beliefs and experiences and they in turn distort the true inner voice so that when we think our intuition is telling us something that is true, it is really a wrong belief we learned when we were young. Over time the practice of meditation clears the way for the voice to speak clearly and accurately without bias or distortion, which is why, in the beginning, it is extremely useful, and often essential, to have the guidance of someone more experienced when learning meditation. This book is your first guide.

Q. *How do I know that this is the right method of meditation for me?*

A. No one can tell you which method is the right one for you. Only you will know through a combination of intuition and experience. You may experience a few moments of peace while gazing into a candle flame but it is unlikely to help you transform a pattern of negative thinking and acting. The rhythm of a mantra being chanted verbally, or even mentally, may suspend anxious and angry thoughts (stress) for a while, but it won't alter the underlying beliefs and perceptions which are responsible for your stressful emotions. Do explore and experiment with methods of meditation, but we recommend that you work with only one method at a time. A good test of any method is to ask yourself five questions: does it increase my self awareness; does it help me understand myself better; does it empower me to transform my deepest negative habits; does it help bring a lighter and more positive energy to my relationships; does it help me 'see' more clearly my values and my purpose in life.

Q. *Is this all meditation is, just a method to relax and be more peaceful?*

A. You could stop at this stage and simply use this initial method of meditation as a physical and mental relaxation exercise. However, it won't help you understand and change the deeper tensions and anxieties which now influence your feelings and your responses to others on a daily basis. That requires a deeper insight into the roots of those anxieties and the inner power to alter transform old habits and tendencies. Insight, understanding and the power to change are some of the results of deepening your meditation as you work through this book. Try not to rush through the book. The first four lessons are like foundation stones. The deeper and stronger they are the easier it becomes as you progress.

A Personal Experience

I don't think I was a natural meditator, whatever that means. I've never been one to sit still easily, especially mentally. If I wasn't doing all the talking, I was certainly doing all the thinking. And then I realised it was draining my energy and I had become quite negative in certain areas. So although I found meditation almost impossible at first, very slowly, almost imperceptibly, it helped me to control my thinking and, over a period of years, has totally changed my quality of life. Not only do I feel better, but other people who have known me for years have commented on how much calmer I am. I feel that my relationships with others have improved and I am far more tolerant than I used to be. When I began to notice changes within myself I could see that my effort was worthwhile.

Journal Exercises

A. Waste Disposal

Write down the main waste or negative thoughts that seem to be interfering with your ability to concentrate your mind. After you have completed your list, take each thought and write it on a small, separate piece of paper. Then tightly crush each paper, imagining that each thought is destroyed in the process, then throw the paper into the waste bin.

B. Creating your Peace Room

Visualise a house and in that house there is a 'peace room'. Visualise the room as an empty space. Then, step by step decorate and finish the room with the colours and objects which symbolise peace to you. See the sun streaming into the room, filling the room with light. Then see yourself sitting in the room and filling the room with your vibrations of peace. This is now your 'inner peace room' and you can go there any time – it takes only a second – and peace awaits you. To keep it fresh in your mind write a description of your peace room.

C. Remaining Peaceful

Think of a person in your family, or a colleague at work, who always manages to 'press your buttons'. Imagine sitting with him/her beside a calm lake. You are both talking peacefully about how you love to lead peaceful lives. Keep this thought and image in your mind daily for one week and mark your progress on a scale of 1-5 (1 being least successful) in the table below

Day	Did I remain peaceful today?	Did I interact peacefully with this person today?	Did I see the quality of peace in this person today?
1			
2			
3			
4			
5			
6			
7			

D. Reviewing the Day

If you scored less than 3 on any day for any of the points above, are you able to identify what prevented you from achieving a higher score? Were you were able to achieve success, are you able to identify what helped you to reach your goal? Note down your experience of doing this exercise and bear your comments in mind as you continue to practise and monitor your own progress.

Who Am I?

Rediscovering the true identity and
nature of the self

Amnesia is the medical condition where there is a sudden and
total loss of memory. Not only does the person not recognise
those people involved in their life, including the closest family
members, they don't even remember their own identity. On learning
of someone suffering from this sudden affliction, most of us have
probably experienced a sense of gratitude that it has never happened
to us. And yet, from a purely spiritual point of view, that is exactly
what has happened to us all. The only difference is that we are not
aware that we have completely forgotten who we are. It's only when
we stop and ask ourselves' "Who am I?" (and stay with the
question) that we discover how we flit between self concepts and
definitions that inadequately describe our true identity.

Encounters with strangers in social settings also illustrate our ignorance of who we are. A series of questions demonstrates that we are eager to find a label or a box into which to fit a new acquaintance. The opening conversation is peppered with the standard questions, "What do you do?" and "Where do you come from?" (or questions of a similar nature, depending on the culture/country where you happen to be). This allows us to identify the other by their vocation and their location, if not their nation, or some other socially accepted norm. Identity is mistakenly based on what you do and where you were born and includes other unspoken labels or boxes such as gender, wealth, looks, politics, sports team, beliefs, religion, race, etc. By the time the 'getting to know you' phase is over, we have the other person neatly wrapped up in a set of labels which gives us the feeling of 'now I know who they are'. And if we were self-aware in that moment, we might have noticed that as we label others so we are labeling and categorising ourselves.

Each label then becomes our identity, depending on where we are, who we are with or what we are doing. If we stand back for a moment and reflect on our experience, we might find that none of these labels are truly what we are. The moment we fall into the trap of thinking we are what we do, where we come from or our status in life, we create feelings of insecurity and there is a sense of vulnerability.

This is what happens. If we say we are what we do, then the moment someone criticises our work, perhaps our paintings or drawings if we are a painter or an architect, then we generate anger and fear towards that person. Why? Because we perceive the criticism to be a personal attack. As a result, we build a wall, a defensive barrier around ourselves, and our behaviour becomes defensive and protective. This is how many people live their life. It is called perpetual insecurity, and it drains our self-esteem. Similarly, we may identify with what we do e.g. our position as managing director at work. When we return home in the evening, unless we consciously release the role of managing director, we may find ourselves trying to be a managing director to our family when they obviously need a father or a mother or a wife or husband. The same happens when we base our sense of identity on our country of physical birth. We become nationalistic and generate fear and animosity towards the people of other nations, even if only in subtle ways. The two main sources of conflict in the world are between people who identify with their belief systems (religion) or the colour of their skin (race). In all these examples we are simply identifying with a label. We are not a label. Neither are we a set of beliefs. Our beliefs come and go, we can change them at will. They can be as impermanent as the clothes we wear if we so decide. If we were to take a few moments to explore human conflict, we might find that all anger and fear, and all the interpersonal and international wars to which they lead, have their roots in this amnesia of the soul. It is simply our forgotten sense of our true self-identity, or mistakenly identifying with what we are not.

If we were to ask ourselves the question, "From all the labels we place on ourselves and use to define ourselves, which one is the real me, the real person – which one truly describes me?", which one would it be? In response to this question, many people say, "They are all me – there is a little bit of them all in me." Essentially we can call this the first sign of an identity crisis. It also means we are all in an identity crisis. We are all suffering from a severe case of 'mistaken identity'. This dis-ease is now so common that we think it's normal. We even identify with personality types and say to

ourselves, "Yes, I am like that", "I'm a bit if a worrier", "I'm the passive aggressive type" "I'm a loner". Out of habit, we have come to believe that we are the accumulation or acquisition of certain personality traits or characteristics. It is this learned misidentification with labels and traits which prevents us seeing and knowing the real self, the true self.

So who or what are we really? In truth, the answer is simple, because the illusion is simple. We make a very simple mistake, which is passed on from generation to generation. We confuse two things, body and soul, or role and identity. We identify with the body we occupy and the roles we play and then depend on our body and our roles for our source of self-esteem and self-worth. If we can see the truth in Shakespeare's perception that all the world is a stage, and all men and women merely players, with many parts to play, we would see that we play many roles but we are not the roles. The self is not the role, the self is the soul. The soul is the actor, the body is the costume. We are all simply actors and each day is filled with many scenes. There is the scene of the lounge at home, the office, the political gathering, the passport control desk at the airport, the supermarket, the football stadium, etc. Each scene requires us to play a different and appropriate role and then, as soon as the scene is over, to drop that role and move on to the next scene. Many people have to play many different and sometimes opposing roles, and when they mistakenly identify with the role they quickly and easily lose the sense of who they are. Others get stuck in one role and cannot understand why they have the feeling that life has them 'boxed in'.

Real freedom comes with enlightenment, and the first enlightenment is the understanding that we are simply actors, and the physical body which we animate is our costume. While the many scenes of life and the many roles we play come and go, we remain. While thoughts and feelings come and go, we remain. Here at the centre of myself is the real I – the conscious, self-aware being, within this physical costume called the human form. Even our body comes and goes, but we remain.

Who Am I... What Am I?

Life is essentially an interplay between two energies – the physical, non-living[3] energy of matter and the living[4] energy of the self or consciousness or soul. The living energy of the soul or self has awareness of its own existence (self-awareness) – we think, judge, decide, remember and desire, but we are not our thoughts, our judgements or desires – whereas the non-living energy of the material body does not do this. The body, with its five senses, is animated by the soul or self, and it is the instrument, temple and vehicle of the soul.

The Great Mistake

From the moment we are born, we are taught to identify with our physical form. We learn to label and compartmentalise others by their form. These false identities lead to a false awareness of ourselves, including boy, girl, man, woman, teacher, engineer, French, British, black, white, Christian, Muslim, etc. When we limit the consciousness of ourselves to a label or compartment, we become protective and defensive of our category. Insecurity becomes our companion. Fear and anger become the currency of our relationships. Furthermore, if we only identify with our body, we become tense and preoccupied by its shape, looks and age. This encourages us to create the habit of comparison, which easily and frequently results in a loss of self-esteem. Real beauty has little to do with our body. We intuitively know this but, in the face of our cultural conditioning and the pressures of modern society, we go along with the prevailing illusion that beauty is what we see in the bathroom mirror in the morning.

This 'misplaced identity' is the great mistake we all make. In truth, the real, original, eternal identity of the self is not based on our body, actions or place of birth, but on our essence as soul.

It is not that I have a soul
somewhere in my body

I am a soul and
I animate this body.

You are also a soul.[5]

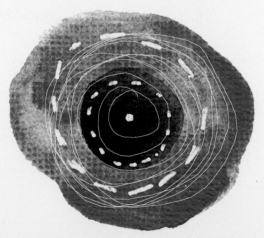

Our Real Form and Location

The soul is a small point of pure, spiritual light which is conscious
and self-aware, whose eternal and true nature is peaceful and full of
love. Located above and behind the eyes, we receive information
about the world through the five senses of our body and the brain. If
you find this hard to understand, just ask yourself quite naturally,
"Where do I do my thinking?" The chances are that, if asked to
point to where your thinking takes place, you would point to an area
somewhere in the middle of your forehead.
The brain is like your computer and you (the soul) are the operator.

This awareness of your self as soul does not diminish the value of
your brain or body in any way. It simply corrects your relationship
with your brain and body. It breaks the spell of self-forgetfulness
and the habit of identification with form.

Soul and Role are Different

Good actors can play any role. They will
play each role to the best of their ability,
but will never actually think, "I am
Romeo" or "I am Juliet." However
involved they are with their roles, at the
end of the performance, they will take off their
costumes, drop the characteristics and traits of the
role and resume their true identities.

The following thoughts can help you break the habit of identifying
with your roles:
*Whatever role I, the soul, am required to play, I maintain my true
self-awareness, my true identity as a soul – a living, spiritual, eternal
being. The body is simply my temporary, physical costume through
which I can create and play as many roles as I wish.*

Our Spiritual Possessions

Just as our true identity is one of spirit, so our true nature is
'spiritual'. The innate characteristics or attributes of the soul are
peace, love, truth, happiness and power. These attributes are ever
present within us: they never leave us and they are as eternal as the
soul itself. However, we lose awareness of their presence within when
we fall under the spell of the illusion that we are what we see in the
mirror (physical form), what we do (profession), where we come from
(race or nationality) or what we have (possessions). When our sense
of self is based on any of these things, we live in perpetual, sometimes
subtle fear, because all these things change or can be threatened –
they come and go and we have no control – and where there is fear
there cannot be peace, love or contentment. This is why
identification with our body, and all material things related to it, is
the root of all our fears, and in turn is the basis of all forms of stress.

Meditation corrects the great mistake we all make by restoring the awareness of our self as a soul, a tiny point of radiant, spiritual light. Practised over a period of time, this awareness naturally leads to an experience of our true nature: a deep inner peace and contentment that is not dependent on anything physical. This is known as the true consciousness of the soul or soul-consciousness. As we become more aware of ourselves as a soul, the one who is performing each action through the body, we gain greater control over our thoughts, feelings, words and actions. The natural consciousness of our self as a peaceful being then fills all our actions; our desire for peace of mind is fulfilled from inside and not outside.

As you begin your meditation, think about your true identity and remind yourself of *who you are as the eternal and imperishable soul.* Create thoughts about the self as a soul, and about your original qualities. If your thoughts wander away, gently bring them back and refocus. The simplest true thought about yourself is the phrase, *"I am a peaceful soul."* As you contemplate and concentrate on this thought, it becomes a real experience. This is what is meant by self-realisation. It happens at the moment you see and experience that all your learned identities (based on what you do, what you believe or where you physically come from) are all illusions and are replaced by the experience of the truth about yourself – *you are a spiritual being, you are a soul occupying a physical body.* When you actually experience this, it can then be said that you are in the consciousness of the soul or soul-conscious.

When you are truly conscious of yourself as soul, you realise that you have nothing to lose. You will gradually understand that everything external cannot be possessed and therefore lost, and you know that you already have the peacefulness, feelings of love and wisdom that you seek. These are the innate and eternal qualities of every soul and while you may lose your awareness of them due to body-consciousness, they can never be taken from you. You also realise that you cannot control any other person or external event. However, you can influence them according to your own thoughts, attitudes and behaviour, which only you can control.

Seven Stages of Meditation to achieve Self-realisation

Meditation is the bridge between the theory of who we are and the experience of who we are. As we learn to cross this bridge there are seven key stages or steps in the process which, in time, will happen automatically and almost instantly. However, at this stage of laying the foundations of your meditation practise it is useful to consciously move though each step:

- **Relax** your body.

- Withdraw your attention from everything around you, including your body.

- **Affirm**, using your thoughts, your identity as a soul or spirit, and your nature as innately peaceful and full of love.

- **Contemplate** the knowledge of yourself as a soul, a point of spiritual light.

- **Concentrate** attention on yourself as a peaceful, loving being.

- **Experience** yourself as a soul and acknowledge the feelings of inner peace.

- **Maintain**, without force, consciousness of yourself as a soul even while in action and interaction with others.

Meditation 2 – Realisation of the Self

The purpose of this meditation is to help you to experience who and what you truly are, soul not body. Don't try to force this. Let your thoughts be slow and gentle.

I sit comfortably and consciously relax my body..

I bring all my attention up through my body to a point in the middle of my forehead just above and behind the eyes...

This is where I, the soul, reside within this body...

I am not this body, I am the one who animates it...

I am the driver and this body is my vehicle...

I am not my eyes and ears – they are my windows onto the world...

I am the dweller, looking out through my windows...

I concentrate my attention on myself...

I ignore any wandering thoughts or distractions...

I begin to experience myself as I really am – a tiny point of concentrated energy that is conscious and self-aware...

I am also aware that I am radiating energy...

I am a being of light, radiating light...

I am the light that is consciousness...

I am the eternal, imperishable light that is the soul...

I contemplate myself as a point of radiant, sparkling light...

And I experience the freedom and the peace that wells up inside as I realise who and what I really am...

I am now in the consciousness of the soul, my original and true consciousness...

Without force, I maintain that consciousness for as long as I can...

When I feel ready, I gently return my awareness to the room around me and this moment now bringing with me the inner peace that I have rediscovered in my meditation.

When you finish your meditation, take a moment to reflect on what you have experienced; note how your inner vibration and perhaps your mood has changed. This validation of your experience helps you to appreciate and value what you are gaining from your meditation practice. Practise this meditation twice a day, for ten minutes each time. Sometimes the effects of meditation can be delayed. You may not feel particularly concentrated, peaceful or aware of yourself as a soul when you are trying to meditate. It may be a couple of hours later when you are suddenly overcome by a wave of inner peace or deep contentment. The delayed fruits of meditation are often the sweetest.

Open your three eyes

This particular method of meditation (Raja Yoga) is best practised with eyes open. If we close our eyes it is a signal to our consciousness and our body that sleep is close and the last thing we want to encourage within ourselves while meditating is falling asleep. Meditation is a way to wake up and stay awake, not only consciously, but in terms of our awareness of what is happening internally and externally. It is therefore good to practise with eyes open as soon as possible so that during your meditation you can become accustomed to going beyond the physical input of what you see as well as what you hear.

By practising with open eyes, it becomes easier to create the right state of consciousness while still being dimly aware of our surroundings. This will be essential in day to day activities when we will want to stay connected to our inner peace while others around us tend to panic. It will also help us to move deeply into our consciousness during conversations which require both depth and clarity of ideas and concepts. This is when we will need our third eye, the eye of our intellect, which gives us the ability to see what is true and false, and to make the right decisions without being influenced by others or our own unruly emotions.

Frequently Asked Questions

Q. *Why is there so much suffering in the world?*

A. The deepest reason why there is so little peace and so much anger and fear in both our personal experience and our human relationships today is because we have lost this awareness of our true identity and true nature. Our identity has become based on physical appearance (body), actions (what we do/the roles we play), possessions (what we accumulate), location (where we physically come from) or conditioning (learned beliefs). When our identity is based on any of these, we spend our life in inner and outer conflict, defending and protecting one of many of these false identities. Fear becomes our companion (fear of loss or damage). This is the core and universal reason for all suffering and conflict in the world today. Our greatest contribution to bringing peace into the world is therefore to recover and restore our inner peace. The method is meditation, and it begins with one vital but simple truth, "I am a soul and my true nature is peace."

Q. *I don't have much time. How often do I need to meditate?*

A. As with anything else, the more we practise, the more we feel the benefit of what we are doing. We do need to practise meditation regularly because the habits of identifying with our physical form and being dependent upon the experience of physical stimulation are deep. We easily slip out of the awareness of the soul and back into consciousness of the body and sensual stimulation. Meditation is not only sitting in a quiet corner going deeply into our own consciousness to connect with our inner source of peace, it is also the way to gently remind ourselves, many times a day, that we are souls, spiritual beings not physical beings. The illusion of being physical is so deeply ingrained that we need to take frequent moments to remember and remind ourselves who we are.

Use the following regularly to remind yourself :

I have a body but I am not my body

I have thoughts but I am not my thoughts

I have feelings but I am not my feelings

I have beliefs but I am not my beliefs

I play many roles but I am not my roles

I am the one who remains at the centre of all that comes into and passes through my life

I am a soul,[6] eternal and imperishable, and my original and true nature is one of peace

Q.   *Even if I do feel a little more peaceful than usual during or after meditating, it doesn't last long. So what's the point?*

A.   It's been quite a while since most of us have experienced true inner peace. It is the kind of peace that is not dependent on any outer stimulation or circumstance. So it may take a little while to rediscover and regain your true inner peacefulness, and it may take a little while longer to learn how to sustain it. And a little while more to be able to maintain it in every scene and situation in daily life. You will slowly discover the reasons why it takes a 'little while', as you continue through the lessons in this book. How long is a 'little while'? There is no right length of time, and our progress should not be measured in time. It simply varies from person to person.

Q.   *If I don't identify with my nationality or profession or family, or with any of those things we are taught to identify with, does it not mean that I will lose my identity?*

A.   It can seem as if you may lose your identity from a theoretical point of view. In fact you have already lost it. All the false, learned identities have been masking your true identity, your true self awareness. When you see and drop all the false identities you regain your true sense of self. Your true self identity is obviously not something you write on your next passport application form! We all speak the universal language of labels, so we learn to describe ourselves according to our labels. But now you know you are not a label and through the practice of meditation you will experience 'for real' that you are simply a being of conscious energy, animating a physical form. In that moment of self realisation, you find a new freedom, an inner freedom, the freedom to be your self!

A Personal Experience

The idea that I was, or should I say I am, an eternal, imperishable being was a revelation to me. As I was walking home after hearing this for the first time it was as if I was walking on air. At last it felt like I had an answer. Although I wasn't exactly sure what the question was at the time, I had an answer. "I'm a soul. I'm a soul." I kept saying to myself: "I'm just a simple soul." And the more I thought about it, the more this one answer resolved hundreds of other questions. And, yes, my peace of mind was real. At last, I could allow myself to be at peace.

Journal Exercises

A. From Peaceless to Peaceful Moments

Reflect for a few moments and write down three situations when you normally lack or lose your peace during the course of the day.

1.

2.

3.

Use the term *om shanti* to mentally invoke your inner peace in each of those situations. (om shanti - I am a soul and my nature is peace) At the end of the day, note down what difference it made to the interaction.

B. Check and Change

Using one of the situations that you identified in Task A, complete the table below for a period of one week (use percentages, 1-5, A-E or whatever system you wish, to quantify your behaviour).

Day	How well did I recognise the situation in advance?	To what degree did I consciously focus on my inner peaceful self?	By how much do I feel that I have changed my usual response to this situation?
1			
2			
3			
4			
5			
6			
7			

C. Review and Renew

Write freely about how you think you are progressing, what seem to be the main obstacles (if there are any) and what you think you need to do more of, less of, or differently to continue progressing.

D. From Role to Soul

List the main roles that you play in your life today, then rank them in order of importance.

Which role do you find most challenging and why?

How do you think meditation may eventually help you to play that role more effectively?

Strengthening Soul-Consciousness

Making meditation practical

The assertion of our true identity as an imperishable and eternal soul is easy to understand at the level of our intellect. Many people say they know that they are a spiritual being having a physical experience and not a physical being having the occasional spiritual experience. They even use the term 'soul' to describe themselves. However, the underlying truth is that very few of us find it easy to experience ourselves as souls. It has been such a long time since we had the awareness of being a soul. Our deepest habit has been to identify with everything that we are not, beginning with our own body, and whatever we identify with, we become attached to. If we think we are our nationality, then we become attached to our national identity and everything connected with it. As a consequence, if someone insults our nation, we immediately experience irritation, or even anger. The next time we see that person, we may experience fear, tension or animosity in their presence, as we recall what they said and worry that they may say it again. As soon as we misidentify with something, we make ourselves emotional slaves to people and events. Obviously that is not the most effective way to live but it is how almost everyone has learned to live, and it goes some way to explaining why health services worldwide are now stretched to the limit. Dis-ease within our consciousness must eventually find expression in some form of disease in our body.

Reaching the state of awareness where we are conscious of ourselves as souls, therefore, requires us to detach and dis-identify. Detachment is not an idea which finds easy acceptance in our modern culture of acquisition and accumulation. Many people feel threatened by the concept of detachment and sense a cold, uncaring approach to life within its meaning. However, at the simplest level, detachment simply means standing back and viewing life from a more distant perspective. Imagine standing on top of a high building, looking down on the streets below. We are far away from the action, observing from a distance and detached from the world below. Notice how we can see a bigger picture, and if we stay free of judgement about what we see, we will be able to interpret what we see with greater calm and clarity. Sometimes we glimpse ourselves on TV in a shop window. Knowing that a camera is recording us, looking at ourselves on the screen gives us a sense of observing ourselves from a distance. There is a feeling that while we are participating fully in life, we are also observing ourselves and our life from the position of a witness. This is detachment.

From a purely spiritual point of view, when we attach our consciousness to anything it is as if we lose our freedom to the object of attachment. If we were to watch our 'self' in the moment of attachment, we would see that we lose our 'self' in the object of attachment. This is why detachment is essential if we are to be free to love and care for others, and be able to discern and decide what form that love should take. When we are attached to an object or a person, it is the inner mental action of being attached which becomes the seed of the fear of loss, damage or change. It is this fear which then leads to other life-draining emotions and attitudes such as anger, envy, jealousy, pride, etc., and when any of these emotions are present, it is not possible to be loving towards others or have a caring nature.

Understanding Detachment

To our conditioned minds it appears to be a paradox, but it is a basic spiritual truth – to be loving it is necessary to be detached. Attachment is the root of fear and fear and love cannot co-exist just as day and night, winter and summer, hot and cold cannot exist at the same time as each other. This understanding of the polarity of love and fear has been at the heart of the world's ancient wisdoms for thousands of years. However, it has been clouded by the modern religion of consumerism and the idea that in order to be happy we must acquire 'things' and form relationships of attachment to them. Our entertainment industries sustain the illusion that in order to find love we must possess or be attached to the other person. This confusion between love and attachment has been translated into all our relationships in a number of ways, including the mother and child relationship. When the mother worries over the late return of the child in the evening, and the child eventually returns, she may tell the child off with words of anxiety: "I was so worried about you." To which the teenager may reply, "Why do you keep worrying about me? I'm fine. Leave me alone!" To which the mother may then say, "It's because I care." But since when has worry been the same as care? If worry is fear and care is love, when did fear become love? However, this particular illusion has been handed down through so many generations that the belief that worry shows that you care is deeply entrenched in human consciousness. The regular practice of meditation raises your awareness of this and many other similar false beliefs, allowing you to see and restore the truth at your own pace.

Worry, anxiety and tension are the most common forms of fear. They always arise from some form of attachment and they not only drain the energy of our consciousness, they will, over time, poison our relationships. Where we find the negative energy of such emotions arising in our life, the solution is always detachment. To help us overcome the fear of loss that is associated with detachment, it is helpful to nurture the truth that possession is an illusion. From a purely spiritual point of view, it is just not possible to possess anything. Everything comes and goes. Everything in life comes in order to pass. In the true state of being conscious of the self as soul, we not only know this but we also experience the transience of everything that is outside ourselves and there is a clear understanding that holding on to anything is futile, a waste of time and energy. If we can arrive at this point of realisation, we are knocking on the door of joy. We are under the illusion that we can take joy from objects, people and places, but in truth joy is something we experience when we put our heart 'into' something and our intention is one of 'giving to' and not 'taking from'. Think of the creative activity in which you experience the greatest joy and you will notice that your joy is coming from inside out not outside in. However, if our heart is attached to something, dependent on something or someone, it will be impossible to experience real joy. Whatever our heart is attached to is blocking the outward flow of our energy. The flow is from outside in, not inside out. And finally, when we are attached to anything it means our mind and heart are busy with our attachments, making sure they 'stay close', and often losing ourselves in them. In this state of consciousness, we are not able to remain open to new things arriving in our life, in fact we are blocking them. Worried minds and closed hearts make it hard to see and receive new ideas, opportunities and even people in our life. In a true state of soul-consciousness we are liberated from the anchors of attachment. When we are aware of ourselves as spiritual beings, we cease to lose our sense of identity in what is not the self. We are able to drop the many false concepts about the self which have been part of our education and conditioning. In doing so we lose nothing real. In fact the opposite is true, we rediscover our real, authentic self. We regain the world, our inner world, and access to our spiritual power.

Practical Benefits of being Soul-conscious

How can the awareness of being a soul help to improve our attitude towards ourselves and others? One of the most powerful habits that we learn early in life is comparing ourselves with others, seeing ourselves in the light of what we consider to be their merits or their weaknesses. This can easily lead to a feeling of hopelessness, self-criticism and lack of self-worth, or to feelings of superiority, where the ego becomes critical of others. Through the experience of soul-consciousness, there is a direct experience of the innate qualities of the soul (peace, love, power). When we realise these spiritual attributes are ever present within the self, we come to realise our own worth and stop comparing ourselves with others. This heals the habits of self-criticism and self-denigration which so many of us learn in our formative years. Any self-doubt and self-limitation are gradually replaced by a true sense of our self-worth and a deeper faith in the self. However, this process of healing the habit of self-criticism, created over our lifetime, can take a little time. Once again, patience with ourselves is important.

When we understand and experience ourselves to be eternal, imperishable beings of spirit, it also changes our vision and awareness of others. We see them in a more equal way and the result is a sense of being part of a large family, a brotherhood[7] of souls. Our spiritual vision deeply influences how we respond to others, especially when others become negative towards us. In the consciousness of the soul we see beyond skin colours and belief systems. Where before we may have returned their negativity and ended in a heated argument, our awareness of the self as soul and the ability to access our peace and positivity, combined with our awareness of the other as soul, helps us to transform the situation. We now understand that they are responsible for their own negative emotions. It is a symptom of their misidentification with their body or some form of attachment (probably to an old and false self-image) which is inducing their fear or anger. Instead of retaliating, we stay connected to our own inner peace, understand the other is suffering due to the same ignorance of their true identity from which we once suffered, and humbly reach out to offer a hand of forgiveness, friendship and enlightenment. We cannot make them take it, but in offering we are saying we value and respect them as kindred spirits, regardless of their behaviour. In this way we can build trust and harmony, and transform our relationships.

There are other ways in which soul-consciousness can help us to help others. We cannot give what we do not have ourselves. When friends come to us in distress, often the most we can do is give sympathy. Although this is reassuring, it is not necessarily very

helpful. When in trouble, what people need most is power and clarity. Some situation has triggered weakness and confusion in their mind, making it difficult for them to see things clearly. If any insights or suggestions we offer them are not only sympathetic, but also filled with peace,

power and practicality, they can then take away not only comfort,
but something which will be of practical and positive value in
helping them to solve their problems. A strong, uncluttered mind is
needed for this – one of the fruits of our daily meditation practice.
We only need to remember that we cannot help others at this level of
spiritual empowerment until we ourselves are empowered. Hence the
need for our own daily meditative and reflective practice.

Having an awareness of the soul also helps us to be easy and natural
in the company of others. This easiness on our part helps them to
relax and they don't feel the pressure of expectation. When we are
in a state of soul-consciousness, we only see the good in others, not
just the apparent virtues, but hidden ones as well. This, in turn,
helps them to realise their own positive qualities and talents. A
deepening love and respect for other souls develops naturally as we
recognise our spiritual kinship. There is the realisation that,
regardless of race, culture and nationality, we are all part of the same
global family, sharing the same world. We are all in the same play,
sharing the same stage. While we are each quite unique, separate,
autonomous, spiritual beings whose essence is love and truth, we are
aware that we are also interconnected on a more subtle level.

From Rational Thinking to Intuitive Thinking

One of our greatest daily challenges is decision-making. The pace of life is such that, unlike previous generations, we all have to make hundreds of small and often many major decisions every day. The process of arriving at a decision or choice can be slow, crude and cumbersome or fast, subtle and light. It is the difference between rational and intuitive thinking. Rational thinking is the measured use of reason, step-by-step logic, weighing possibilities and probabilities, often drawing on experience to arrive at a rational conclusion. On the other hand, intuitive thinking is listening to that still, small voice of our innate wisdom which speaks to us from deep within our consciousness. It is instantaneous and requires no logical or rational explanation. The voice of intuition is speaking to us all the time, trying to guide us, but we are not quiet enough to hear it. Negative thoughts, painful memories, learned misperceptions all 'crowd out' our ability to hear. A word of caution here: our intuition is not always right as it can sometimes be influenced by misconceptions! Meditation quietens the mind and memories, and gives us the inner silence to listen and be led by our wisdom and our conscience. In time we can grow to fully trust that voice again. There will always be a place for rational or logical thinking, especially in the practical aspects of living, however, our intuitive capacity will serve us better in all matters of spirit, most especially in our own spiritual awakening and development.

Relaxing into being Soul-conscious

It seems that the stress which comes with modern living inhabits all corners of our consciousness and all areas of our lives. Many people consider being able to relax at will an achievement in itself. Making meditation a natural part of our life, with its practical benefits, is the deepest form of relaxation. Ultimately, it is not so much something that we do, but more a way of creating our state of being. While the deepest levels of soul-consciousness mean our thoughts are slow and peaceful, the secret of staying relaxed in the practical situations of everyday life is to ensure that our mind always has soul-conscious thoughts.

The art of relaxation does not lie in any physical exercises or postures but in the posture of our minds. Essentially there are five levels or qualities of thoughts which we can create:

- **Necessary thoughts**, such as, "I must not forget to go to the supermarket today", or "I have to collect the children from school at 4 pm."
- **Waste thoughts**, which include worrying about things that might not happen, and thoughts about others that spill out as gossip.
- **Negative thoughts**, which include feelings of anger, fear, doubt, sadness, regret and unease. Negative thoughts make us lazy[5] and drain our energy.
- **Positive thoughts**, which are affirmative and focused, carrying only the best intentions for ourselves and for others.
- **Soul-conscious thoughts** arise from the truth of who and what we are, and require the effort of remembering and gently reminding ourselves that we are eternal souls and our real nature is peaceful and loving. When we stay connected to our true state of soul-consciousness, then the energy we share with

others through our thoughts, feelings and attitudes will be
coloured by acceptance, care and compassion – just three of the
many expressions which our love can take. When we restore
our awareness of self as soul, it allows us to clearly see and
release any negative or waste thoughts. This requires a form of
inner vigilance at first, until a natural awareness and sustenance
of soul-consciousness is established. Once again, the qualities of
patience and quiet determination will help us here.

Once we are aware of the possible types of thoughts, then we are in a
position to monitor our thoughts and understand where our energy is
being wasted. Once we recognise that there is a pattern of waste and
negative thinking, usually triggered (not caused) by certain situations
or people, we can then interrupt the pattern and break the pattern of
'habit thinking', thereby changing this waste of energy into
something more positive. Eventually, as we become more practised
at being soul-conscious, patterns of positive thinking will establish
themselves with a power that cannot be diminished, regardless of the
situations or the people we face.

Meditation 3 – Keeping it Simple and Guiding Yourself

During your meditation, keep your thoughts and themes simple – two or three carefully chosen ones are enough. Repeat them gently, giving yourself plenty of time to explore the feelings behind them. Allow your thoughts to develop as you now guide yourself in your meditation. For the next few days, take up two or three simple themes or phrases as the foundation for your own personal meditation. While listening to a guided meditation commentary on tape or CD can be helpful in the early practice of meditation, we encourage you to start creating your own powerful, positive thoughts. These will ultimately have more meaning for you and you will more easily be able to relate to them. However, on your way to reaching a more confident stage, here are a few ideas to help you.

- I am a subtle point of consciousness, which resides within this body. I bring this body to life every day, but I am not this body. I am the energy which uses this body to see, to speak and to hear.

- I am a soul, a being of light, radiating pure light into my body, out towards others and the world. As I turn within and remember who I am, I experience my own capacity to have pure love for all others. It is a benevolent love that neither wants nor needs anything in return.

- I am a being of radiant light, like a star in the night sky reflecting and radiating light in the darkness of the night. The light which emanates from the heart of me is peaceful and loving. I know not who it touches, but I know it does touch. It is my gift to the world.

- I am just a tiny point of pure energy, of light. And within that tiny point lie all my thoughts and my personality traits. Within the point of light that I am, lie all the qualities of spirit that I have – I am a source of love, a source of peace, a source of contentment and wisdom.

- I am a conscient point of energy and I give life to my body. This body may be heavy, but I the soul am so light and free that I can almost fly. I experience joy as the soul releases itself from the chains of matter. I am a point of pure spiritual energy, a point of pure light.

- While the world around me is always changing, while even thoughts and feelings come and go, I the soul remain here at the centre of my self, still, unchanging and totally stable. In this inner space of stillness I experience pure peace, pure calm, pure silence.

Repeat and expand these thoughts gently to yourself, allowing them to take root deeply in your mind while enjoying the flowering of the real feelings they bring. It sometimes helps to write them down and then to contemplate them in quiet moments. In this way, you can reconnect with your spiritual power with ease. Remember, the ultimate aim is to go beyond thoughts into the actual experience. But you cannot force this – if you try to, it will not happen. Use the thoughts to gently guide you there. They will fall away of their own accord and, when the time is right, instead of thinking about peace you will reside in peace – the peace which always resides within you.

Retreating

When they encounter the benefits of meditation for the first time, perhaps at a workshop or on a course, some people feel that, in order to get their mental house in order and become more 'spiritual', they need to leave the hustle and bustle of modern living behind and head for the hills. There, they think they will find the time and space to practise meditation and do their inner work. Nothing could be further from the truth. While going on an occasional spiritual retreat is certainly beneficial and highly recommended for our meditation and spiritual development, the real workshop is life itself. It is in the office, car, kitchen, lounge and through our daily interactions with others that we receive the opportunity to practise being soul-conscious, to connect with our inner peace and power and to maintain our spiritual awareness. It is in the mirror of our relationships that we are able to measure our progress. Ultimately, when we are in a true state of soul-consciousness, no person or situation can disturb or harm us.

Meditation 4 – Still Point Watching

Every moment of every day is an opportunity to strengthen your ability to be soul conscious. The practical application of meditation means that you can move into this awareness wherever you are - in the middle of the meeting, during a journey, in the silent spaces of a conversation or simply sitting in a waiting room. These are the basic steps to practise moving into a state of stillness and focusing your awareness.

Sit in a comfortable but alert position wherever you are right now...
Imagine your whole body is surrounded by a shell of subtle light...
See the light draw itself up to a point of focus above and behind your physical eyes...
Be aware that you are that point of focus...
Just as you might stand absolutely still as you look through the
   windows of your home onto the countryside or a street
      outside...look through your eyes now as if they were windows...
         Be aware that you are not your eyes... you are the still point of
            awareness looking through your eyes to the world 'out there'...
Remain still inside while expanding your awareness to hold the whole scene in front of you...
As you watch people and life moving around you, remain completely still...just watching without thinking about what you see...
Then, in one split second narrow your awareness to one small detail in the scene...
Hold that detail for a moment...
Be free of any judgment or assessment, don't project anything onto what is in your awareness...
Just watch...just be aware...
Then expand your awareness to hold the whole room once again...
Remind yourself of who you are...the soul looking out through the windows of the eyes...completely still....focussed...fully aware.

Frequently Asked Questions

Q. *How can I really understand and experience this idea of soul-consciousness?*

A.   The aim of meditation is to experience soul-consciousness. This is a state of awareness that is only possible when you cease to identify with or become attached to anything in your mind. Ultimately it will feel as if your mind is empty, vacant, totally free and yet you are totally aware. Initially the aim is to slow down your thoughts and create the right kind of thoughts based on who you are, then to contemplate those thoughts. The very idea of this inner process can be threatening for many of us. For so long our minds have been 'occupied' with something and we have become occupied with what is on our mind, but once you are able to detach from the thoughts and images on your mind you are struck by how you had become so comfortable with thoughts about limited and negative things. You become aware of how much time and energy you had been wasting and how easily your habitual thoughts, ideas and concepts can suddenly seem like the bars of a self-inflicted prison. As your meditation practice becomes more natural you more easily recognise how you often escape into certain thoughts, concepts and even philosophies, in order to avoid yourself. There is the illusion of thinking that you are thinking deliberately, cleverly and freely, but in truth you entrap yourself with the same thoughts, usually in cyclic processes, every day. Meditation is the way to 'see' this self-entrapment each day and then set yourself free. It restores your ability to consciously use the faculty of your mind for that for which it was designed, the creation and sustenance of right thinking based on truth and love.

Q.   *Why is it that I can't change the pattern of my thoughts so easily?*

A.   Imagine a bird being so comfortable in its nest that, though perhaps occasionally standing on the branch to puff its chest and rustle its feathers, it never wants to fly and does not even realise it could fly. It never knows the exhilarating freedom of flight, never feels the wind through its wings. It thinks the other birds who are flying around are stupid. In much the same way, we never really leave the nest. Our habitual thoughts become our comfort zone and each repetitive thought pattern is like a twig in the nest. We never know our own unlimited nature, feel the breeze of true freedom through our spirit or see the stunning beauty of our own being. Even the thoughts, "I am a soul" and "I am a peaceful being" have to be released eventually, so that we can actually experience their deepest truth.

In the inner world of spirit, thoughts are like the map, but they are not the territory nor the reality of the experience. Thinking "I am a soul" is not being soul-conscious, but it is an essential start. Maps are important and necessary, until we know the way home by heart.

Q.   *You mention the necessity of learning detachment if we are to meditate successfully, but what is the point of being detached? Surely we still have to get involved with people even if we are practising meditation? Does detachment not mean withdrawing from our relationships?*

A.   At the heart of almost all wisdom paths down through the ages is the idea and the practice of detachment. This is simply because one of the deepest habits we learn to develop is attachment and we don't realise that whatever we become attached to becomes a trap for our consciousness, for the self/soul. We know that we are attached when we start thinking about someone or something when they are not present with us and when there is no need to think about them. Our mental energy is being drained and we feel we do not have control over our thoughts and feelings.

Whenever we become attached to anything, we automatically invite fear to be present. Whether it is to people, position, power, pay or even an opinion, any form of attachment means there will be a fear of damage or loss. Fear is the core negative emotion. It takes many faces (worry, anxiety, tension) as it stunts our spiritual growth and chases love away. Detachment is the basis of our capacity to remain positive and loving towards others while interacting with them. This is known as detached involvement and it begins with what is known as a spiritual skill, the ability to be a 'detached observer'.

Q.   *How can I be a detached observer without feeling that I am cold?*

A.   Being a detached observer has two dimensions – the inner and the outer. The inner art of detached observation is the ability to stand back from our own thoughts, emotions, attitudes and behaviour. We are creators and our thoughts, emotions and attitudes are our creation. In fact, this is the first step to self-empowerment. As long as we fail to detach from our thoughts and emotions then they will be our masters and they will drain our energy. Practise simply being the witness of whatever you are thinking and feeling. This is essential to your meditation practice and after a while you will find it both liberating and empowering.

On the external level, the art of detached observation is the art of being a witness to the scenes around us. As we stand back and watch the play of life happen around us, without being actively involved, we can see the 'big picture' more clearly This makes it easier to discern clearly what part we need to play and the most appropriate contribution that we can make.

Q. *What am I supposed to do when friends come to me for emotional support?*

A. Detached involvement is the art of not consuming or being affected by the emotions of others. If a friend or colleague is upset and we also get upset (because they are our friend), we cannot help them see why they are reacting emotionally and how they might change the nature of their emotions by themselves. We simply add fuel to their fire. By remaining detached, we can be more effective in our ability to care, listen and help them reflect on the situation. We can encourage and empower them to change their negative reaction to a more positive response, and thereby generate a healthier energy. If we become over-involved in someone else's problems, there is a risk that our own judgment will be clouded. This is why it is seldom effective to make decisions and choices under the influence of your own and others' emotions.

Q. *I get upset when people do not meet my expectations. What can I do to avoid this?*

A. We can only achieve a neutral stance when we develop the art of expecting the best from others, but not becoming offended or upset when they do not achieve or do what we expect. In this way our vision is always positive and we can remain stable and encouraging when our expectations are not met instantly. It allows us to understand why others were not able to achieve what was expected and to help them overcome any obstacles. We are unable to do this if we ourselves are in a state of disappointment at not having our own expectations met.

Q.   *I worry about whether or not I am making progress. How can I possibly live without having an aim in my life?*

A.   First of all, we need to be detached from the outcomes in our life. We need to develop the art of having a clear goal while not becoming upset or feeling down if we do not achieve it instantly. Our happiness is not dependent on the achievement of an aim or goal. It is good to have aims and goals but not good to make our happiness dependent on achieving them. Happiness is the way to achieve our aims and goals in life, not the result - hence the saying that 'the journey is the destination'. Meditation helps us to stay grounded and focused in the moment called 'now' and to break the habit of delaying our happiness to the moment of achievement which is always 'then'.

A Personal Experience

One of the hardest tasks for me was making decisions. I would frequently feel paralysed when faced with some choices. I realised this was due to the worry or fear of doing the wrong thing or going the wrong way. My mind was full of 'but what ifs' and I just could not see clearly. Meditation gradually (and I mean gradually) helped me to let go of this 'but what if' habit of thinking. I went deeper than these thoughts and enjoyed a bit of inner peace and quiet. This gave me the idea of allowing. I began to allow things to happen instead of feeling I should make them happen. So when I faced any tricky decisions, I put the choices to myself then allowed the inner response to happen. I began to get answers, sometimes subtle feelings, sometimes 'eureka' moments, and the more I followed them the more confidence I began to have in them. I think this is called intuition.

Journal Exercise

A. Spiritual Vision

There is an old saying, "What you spot is what you got". It reminds
us that what we see in others we already have within ourselves. A
spiritual vision in the context of our relationships means we see the
highest spiritual qualities in others despite what they say or do. This
is difficult until we are able to see the same in ourselves. This simple
exercise is a a beginning. Write down the names of three people you
know (family, friend, colleague) and then three positive qualities that
you see in each of them.

1.

2.

3.

B. Now You

Now imagine they are doing the same with you – what would they
write down for you – write nine positive attributes you think they
would see in you.

Regularly affirm your spiritual attributes and the character traits
which they generate. The more you learn to see them within
yourself, the more you will see and appreciate them in others.

C. To Appreciate Not Depreciate

Proof of seeing the best in others is shown when we naturally thank and praise rather than criticise those with whom we interact on a daily basis. Keep a record of your progress in this area, using the table below.

Day	Name of person and relationship	How did I thank or praise him/her?	What was this person's response?
1			
2			
3			
4			
5			
6			
7			

D. Progress Report

Remember that although you may be constantly positive with others, constantly seeing their innate spiritual attributes, it may take time for them to be able to do the same. How long? No one can know. Draw a symbol or picture to show how you have changed your awareness this week.

Aspects of Consciousness

The shaping of personality and understanding the relationship between mind, intellect and sanskaras[9]

E ach and every one of us is an imperishable and eternal soul. Physical death is, therefore, only the ending of one lifetime and the transition to the next. As souls, we take rebirth in a new body, opening a new chapter on our unique and individual journey. Death can be seen as liberation and a new beginning.

It is obviously not possible to prove this scientifically, as science requires physical evidence and, as souls, we are non-physical. However, there are now many books which contain numerous personal stories of out-of-body experiences (OBEs) and near death experiences (NDEs), in which people recount their experience of the existence of the self/soul as separate from the body. Many of us have a memory of such experiences within our subconscious which resonates with such stories. Many others recall past lives under

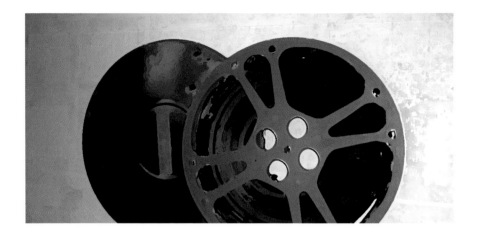

hypnosis, in dream states and in meditation. As you practise meditation and make further progress in experiencing the consciousness of the soul, you will naturally come to experience your own sense of eternity and your undying, peaceful, pure nature – not so much in specific images, more at the level of intuition and insight.

Both the understanding and the experience of having been in different bodies in previous births begin to answer many important questions. One of the most interesting questions is, "Why do we all have such different personalities?" From the day they are born, even twins have completely different personalities. The answer is that we carry with us, from one birth to the next, the subtle traces of personality or character that have been developed in previous births. One of the aims of meditation is to consciously choose and develop the character traits which we want within our personality. This takes place through the interplay of the three main subtle 'instruments'[10] of the soul – mind, intellect and sanskaras. Understanding how these inner instruments work and using each one in the right way is an essential aspect of meditative practice. If we are not the masters of our mind, intellect and sanskaras, they will be the masters of us and meditation will be impossible.

Restoring Self-sovereignty[11]

In much the same way as our body has arms and legs to negotiate the physical world, we have non-physical tools to negotiate the non-physical world of beliefs, values, perceptions, thoughts, feelings, decisions and attitudes. These three faculties of consciousness – mind, intellect and sanskaras – are not separate from the soul but can be seen as integral to the soul. At the same time the soul can consciously use any one of these inner faculties or tools.

Self-sovereignty means that we rule the 'inner kingdom' of our consciousness. When all is well in the 'inner kingdom', we are the rulers of our mind, intellect and sanskaras. They are under our command. When we lose our original and true self-awareness as spiritual beings, we also lose control of our thoughts and feelings (mind) and we are constrained by our many habits (sanskaras). As a result of our loss of soul-consciousness, external dependencies and attachments influence our thoughts and actions and we are no longer sovereign rulers over our own senses. In ancient Indian lore there is one image which describes this loss of self-control. It is the image of the chariot being pulled wildly out of control by five horses. The charioteer is the soul, the chariot is the body and the horses represent the five senses. It depicts our slavery to sensual experiences. It is as if the senses now command the soul.

If we are to be the masters of our own experience, life and destiny, we need to learn how to control and use these faculties of our consciousness. Meditation serves to help us see how they work together, how to use them in the right way and how to empower them.

Why very few human beings are rulers of the self

If we accept that, as pure energy, the soul takes rebirth, then we are able to understand that in our first birth we are pure beings. We bring no impressions of previous lives and therefore no strong internal personality traits or latent habits to influence our thoughts and emotions. In this state of spiritual newness or purity, we express an innocence and playfulness in a world which also appears completely new to us. The expression of the light of each soul is a natural outpouring of the purest qualities of spirit – full of love, joy, generosity – we are constantly content within ourselves and with the world. Sorrow and pain have not yet appeared in our repertoire of experiences. Our relationships are defined by the exchange of this pure energy through our actions and interactions, as we play and dance together, through our eyes, through our mind and heart without obstacle or fear. Many souls have a deep memory of these experiences within their subconscious. The presence of this subconscious memory of our spiritual childhood also helps us to explain and understand the yearning and searching of the human soul for real joy and happiness in life today, and the frustration of finding only pale shadows of such pure joy in limited sensual pleasures. We can only search for what we have once known, but lost.

If a light bulb is connected to a battery and left permanently on without being recharged, gradually the light becomes dim and eventually fades away completely. Only the bulb is seen. In a similar way, the soul expresses and emits its energy through the actions of the mind and the body. The light of our consciousness, and therefore the qualities of joy and love,

slowly diminishes over time and during many births. The only
difference is that the inner darkness, which will eventually pervade
our consciousness, comes not so much from the running down of the
battery of spirit, but more from being swathed in the gradual
accumulation of experiences and impressions, the influences of other
embodied souls and from the world around us. There is always light
and power emanating from within the human soul, but it is
diminished in both intensity and purity by this gradual
gathering of physical experiences which leave layers of
impressions and memories enfolded one within the other, like
the petals of a rose that has not yet flowered.

Over time, the soul, which was originally innocent, pure and
completely open, loses awareness of the self and the purity of
consciousness is corrupted by the influences and stimuli of the
physical world outside. Innocence is lost and the gates of the heart
are closed by fear and sorrow.

The interface between being and doing (soul and action) is the mind.
The mind is not separate from the soul or consciousness; it is the
main faculty of the soul through which all thought is created. As the
layers of impressions gradually encrust themselves around the soul,
and the habits of taking peace and happiness from physical sensation
take root, there begins the occurrence of occasional moments of
amnesia or loss of self-awareness, as if the soul loses a clear sense of
its own identity – we could liken this to a type of absent-mindedness.
The soul falls under the illusion that it is the body, and that peace
and happiness have physical, sensual sources outside in the physical
world. The spiritual illness of 'body-consciousness' has begun and
gradually grows stronger, spreading to others like an infectious
disease, until every soul believes it is the body which it inhabits. To
a soul that now thinks it is the body, happiness, love, beauty and joy
seem to lie somewhere outside in the world, even in the shape and

form of the body itself – both its own and those of others'. Then, as attachment and dependency (to the physical external stimuli) take root within the soul, control over the self is completely lost and the soul becomes a slave to sensual stimulation. This in turn leads to fear (insecurity) and anger, the two negative emotions which constitute the emotional base of all forms of stress. This then results in the attitudes and behaviours of separation, defensiveness, aggression and conflict.

The exact time that each of us takes to make this journey from pure self-awareness to total spiritual amnesia is not too important at this stage. Only that it takes several lifetimes. Body consciousness, or misidentification with what we are not, is now a spiritual condition which affects every human being in the world. The evidence is there to see in all forms of conflict and where organisational hierarchies attempt to control others. Almost every political, commercial and religious institution suffers from this disease to some extent. When we are body-conscious, thinking that we are the form we inhabit, we give birth to ego within our consciousness. Ego is simply the self/soul misidentifying with something (or someone) that it is not! This can be an object, an idea, perhaps a philosophy or learned belief system and it can last for seconds or for years. When ego is seen and understood from this spiritual point of view, it is always unhealthy and recognised to be the root of all sorrow and suffering, anger and greed, fear and conflict.

Every soul loses its sense of spiritual identity and every souls awareness gradually dims. From our original purity as beings of spirit we have absorbed many impurities. We only have to look within ourselves right now and see the interrelationship and interconnections of our own mind, intellect and behaviour, to experience the truth of our current lack of self-mastery and our diminished spiritual capacities. Looking within and seeing the relationship between our mind, intellect and sanskaras is essential if we are to heal the spiritual scars of identification gathered over many lifetimes, and restore our true spiritual self-awareness. Once again, meditation is the method to 'see' and 'understand' at a pace that suits us individually, and in a way that is kind and gentle to ourselves.

The Mind

The faculty of creation, through which we create all our thoughts which then stimulate or trigger certain feelings.

If our identity and self-awareness is based on the physical (body-consciousness) then the most common form of thought within our mind will be desire. The most frequently used expression will be, "I want!" This habit of 'wanting' is born because we learn to believe that peace and happiness come from outside the self and experienced through our physical senses. Whereas, when we have restored our sense of self as soul (soul-consciousness), we will be content with who we are and what we have, for we will have realised that what we seek we already have within us. Love, peace and happiness are inner states not stimulations. When we experience these spiritual attributes within ourselves, through our meditation practice, we cease to crave them through experiences of the world outside; our thoughts are transformed from a queue of restless desires into peaceful and contented thoughts. Thoughts which are stable and positive then radiate vibrations of the highest quality into the world around us.

The Intellect

The faculty of discrimination and decision-making, which we use to assess right from wrong, good from bad and then make a choice/decision.

When we are body-conscious, it means that we will be attached to many things such as our position, power, possessions, pay, people, our own ideas and beliefs, etc. These attachments mean that we are constantly distorting the energy of our consciousness into the emotions of fear and anger. It is these emotions which then hijack our intellect and stop us from discerning clearly and correctly what is right and wrong. This constant inner emotional noise of anxiety and irritation (the seeds of fear and anger) do not allow us to hear the deepest part of our intellect, which is our intuition. When we are soul-conscious, we are free from attachment and therefore fear. Our consciousness is calm, concentrated and keenly aware of the quiet, but extremely wise voice of our intuition (inner wisdom). Decision-making is easier and choices are made out of wisdom rather than fear. Meditation is the method to put aside our mental attachments and allow us to connect with the wisdom in our heart. A practical demonstration of this is when you decide not to argue with someone any more. You let go of the attachment to 'my belief', which then allows you to listen to the heart of the other (their feelings) and share what's true in your heart (your feelings).

The Sanskaras

*The impressions or recordings of all the actions we have
performed (mental and physical) and the basis of our
personality/character traits today.*

When we are body-conscious over a period of time, we begin to
believe that happiness and love come only with certain external
conditions and are essentially physical, sensual experiences. As we
develop the habits of taking and grabbing, possessing and
accumulating (to one extent or another), then greed sets up camp
within the soul. These negative habits then become traits
(sanskaras) within our nature, and we justify having them
by saying: 'They are a natural inclination and therefore
human nature' – forgetting that we nurtured them. We
cannot see, and often do not want to see, that our greed
and attachment, frustration and worry are learned
behaviours and can therefore be unlearned.

The experience of soul-consciousness transforms our
nature from taking to giving. We realise, and more
importantly experience, that we already have within us
what we seek (love, peace, truth) and that the energy of
spirit is more powerful than that of matter. We know that what we
give, we get back[12] and, when we give love, care and attention to
others and the world, it comes back on all levels, including the
material.

While some of our sanskaras (character traits and tendencies) were
formed from inside out, many are formed from outside in. Inside out
sanskaras and character traits are born of our own beliefs and
perceptions, some of which we have absorbed from others (parents,
teachers, friends) and have made our own. Other inside out

sanskaras have been developed from our own life experiences as we reacted to people and events. Outside in sanskaras, on the other hand, are developed when we simply imitate others, copying their character traits and actions in early life and allowing them to take root within our own consciousness.

The Interaction of Mind, Intellect and Sanskaras

The circular fashion in which these three faculties of the soul work together can be illustrated by looking at how habits are formed, a process that has been well documented in cognitive psychology and other models of consciousness. For example, if you are a smoker, here is what happens when you first encounter cigarettes. As you watch others smoking (and surviving) you might think: 'I would like to try a cigarette.' Your intellect assesses the rightness of the thought. Based on the evidence of others surviving and seemingly enjoying smoking, you make a decision to have a cigarette, which leads to the action of smoking the cigarette. This creates an impression or memory within the soul, rather like cutting a groove in a piece of wood. This groove in the soul (in your consciousness) becomes a tendency or trait and is known as a sanskara. Within the groove is recorded the memory of, firstly, the action of smoking and, secondly, the feelings of stimulation and then relaxation. Whenever you encounter some pressure or a tense situation, this sanskara is stimulated and the memory of the action and feelings emerge in the mind triggering the thought (desire): 'I want to have another cigarette.' The intellect assesses the thought, calling on the evidence of feelings of relaxation and pleasure, and then makes the decision that it is OK to have another cigarette.

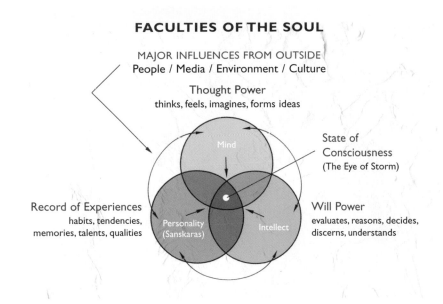

FACULTIES OF THE SOUL

MAJOR INFLUENCES FROM OUTSIDE
People / Media / Environment / Culture

Thought Power
thinks, feels, imagines, forms ideas

Mind

State of
Consciousness
(The Eye of Storm)

Record of Experiences
habits, tendencies,
memories, talents, qualities

Personality
(Sanskaras)

Intellect

Will Power
evaluates, reasons, decides,
discerns, understands

The further action of smoking deepens the sanskara. Every time we smoke we strengthen the memory of smoking and the resulting feelings of relaxation. The recording becomes deeper and stronger. Eventually the intellect is bypassed and we go straight from thought to action. Smoking becomes an automatic response to any tension and a habit is formed. This is how all our habits and tendencies are created and together they constitute our character or personality.

Understanding how our present character traits and tendencies are formed allows us to both see the possibility of change and to begin the process of creating our traits and tendencies based on our true self-awareness as soul, instead of the false awareness of the body. In meditation we experience soul-consciousness and that gives us access to the true underlying nature of the soul, which is love, truth and peace. As we emerge these spiritual qualities and allow them to shape our thoughts, feelings and actions, and therefore sanskaras, they replace the old traits and tendencies, which were created out of body-conscious states of fear, anger and sadness.

In Summary

Meditation is the process of healing the internal wounds caused by the two main illusions which influence the self/soul. Firstly, that we are only physical beings and, secondly, that love and happiness can only be achieved through our physical senses. When we allow these illusions to influence our actions we go against the grain of the self/soul leaving an impression (sanskara) on our consciousness. During meditation the illusions are dispelled and spiritual healing takes place; there is the rediscovery and realisation of the truth of who we are and what we are, which then releases our own spiritual energy and restores soul-consciousness. The natural inclination of the soul, which is not to take in, but to give out, is restored. As we reawaken and mobilise our own spiritual qualities and start to be more loving, we are the first to experience that spiritual love on its way out. We then begin to see why our relationships are important in the process of self-awakening and self-transformation. It is only in the context of our relationships that we can know ourselves and learn how to give of ourselves. In our relationships we find the creative opportunity to express our peacefulness, our feelings of love and joy, thus reversing the flow of our energy in our life from outside in to inside out. In this subtle, inner movement we discover we already have both what we want and what we need! We are already made of a love that cannot be unmade, only lost in the mists of the many illusions, which over time we have allowed to spread through our consciousness.

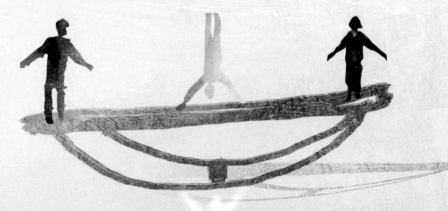

Exercising and Empowering the Intellect

It has been said that for around 80% of our daily lives we are
creatures of habit. This means that most of the time we go straight
from thought to action, without assessing the quality and rightness of
our thoughts. In this way, we bypass the intellect, missing out our
capacity to discern right from wrong and to make conscious
decisions. Our task now is to reawaken and empower the intellect.

Experiment

- In your meditation, withdraw your attention from everything
  around you. Bring yourself back to a point of self-awareness
  and soul-consciousness. Now explore the faculties of your
  consciousness to see how they work together.
- Create a simple thought in your mind. Focus on that thought.
  Concentrate on it. Then use your intellect to assess to
  what degree the thought is right or wrong, and to discern the
  quality of that thought (is it a negative thought, a waste
  thought, a necessary thought, etc.?). If you decide it is
  not a good thought, drop it and create a better thought. In this
  way, you consciously exercise control of your mind and
  intellect. This will eventually restore your feeling of self-
  sovereignty and strengthen your mental and intellectual
  capacities.
- If thoughts or images come from your memories or from
  sources outside your own mind while you are doing this inner
  work, don't give them any energy. Let them go and bring your
  attention back to your own conscious creation.
- Once you have mastered this in your meditation, try the same
  process as you carry out your responsibilities and actions
  throughout the day.

Meditation 5 – Transforming Old Habits

In this exercise, we will select a habit or sanskara, which we do not want, and replace it with a trait which we would like to incorporate as a strand in the fabric of our personality.

I am aware of the unwanted habit of becoming impatient..
As I sit in meditation, I relax my body and become the observer of my own thoughts and feelings...
Affirming my true identity as soul, I remember my real nature is one of calmness, peace and power...
I focus on the power of peace, inviting it and welcoming it into my thoughts and feelings from deep within ... enjoying the calm contentment which it brings...
Then, on the screen of my mind, I begin to visualise patience...
I see myself in a situation where I normally become impatient...
I now see myself as being completely full with the attribute of patience...
I shape my feelings around the idea and image of patience
...unhurried and relaxed... calm and watchful...
If necessary, I can wait ...forever...
I am free of the desire for certain outcomes...
I see how I respond with patience...
I see the effect of my patience on others within the situation...
I now know how I will speak with patience, walk with patience and act patiently in the reality of the situation...
I end my meditation by acknowledging my inner peace of spirit as the mother of my newly created patient attitude.

Frequently Asked Questions

Q.   *I really want to stop the habit of smoking, but I find it hard to stop. Why is that?*

A.   For many smokers, the act of smoking is an unwanted habit, but they find it hard to stop. It is easier to be a slave to the habit and allow the habit to take over their thoughts and decision-making process. The habit started because a cigarette initially provided a physical stimulant that induced temporary feelings of peace and contentment in a tense situation. Or, as children, we smoked because it was a way of enhancing our self-esteem by imitating grown-ups. We now need the power to change this habit and any other habits of dependency or negativity we may have developed. One of the consequences of forgetting who we really are is the development of an addictive personality. We are always wanting, looking, searching outside ourselves for love, peace and contentment; sometimes in subtle ways where we compromise our own feelings and beliefs to please others, hoping for the return of love; sometimes in not-so-subtle ways where we search for power, position or fortune. We each find them in different places, substances or people. But they are brief experiences which are not sustainable in a fast, transient, uncontrollable, external environment. The result is dependency and submission to both the source of stimulation and to the habit itself. As we have seen in this lesson, meditation allows us to find within our consciousness what we seek outside in consumption and dependency. It simply takes a little time to replace the external stimulant with the internal resource. A little patience is required. However, the result is an experience of inner peace and happiness which generates a deep sense of contentment with oneself and the world. The quality of that contentment surpasses any that can be induced from any form of physical consumption. It is a contentment that is without price.

Q. *You mention that we need the power to change. What do you mean by power and where do I find this power?*

A. Recall from Lessons One and Two that at the core of the soul there is a pure, spiritual energy of peace, love, truth and non-dependent happiness. Awareness and experience of this energy provide us with the inner strength needed to change.

Meditation is the method to access and allow this energy to come to the surface of our consciousness and into our minds to colour our thoughts and feelings. In much the same way as hot, molten lava flows from the core of the Earth to the surface through a volcano, we can create volcanoes of power when we meditate. Note, though, that we want to use our energy in a positive way: we are not seeking the kind of power that manipulates and causes damage. When we experience our own source of inner peace, we essentially become free of any dependency on external sources and substances for feelings of contentment and calm. When we generate our own feelings of love and self-acceptance, we cease to be dependent on others and our addiction to their acceptance and approval diminishes and eventually disappears. When we generate our own feelings of contentment within ourselves, we become free from the need for substances, places or physical experiences in order to be happy.

Using this inner power in the right way allows us to let the old addictive habits within our personality atrophy and eventually die. Any unwanted habit can be changed and the scars of all the negative habits, which have developed within the soul over a long period of time, can be healed.

Q. *How can I understand better the reason for wanting to be 'soul-conscious'?*

A. Are you aware that whenever you lose your true self-awareness (soul-consciousness), you will identify with and get attached to something that is not you? It could be another person, your job, or some possession. Let's say you are attached to your job and one day, due to the restructuring of your organisation, you are asked to leave. The attachment to and identification with your position, which has become a habit (sanskara), stimulates the creation of fearful and angry thoughts (e.g., "I'm going to lose my job" or "How dare they change the organisation and jeopardise my position"). The destructive energy of these thoughts becomes emotion (energy in motion) which then invades your entire mind so you cannot have clear and calm thoughts. It hijacks your intellect so you cannot make well-informed, wise decisions and choices. Any connection you had with your inner peace is broken. All this happens because you forgot who you really are and had begun to think you are what you do. When seen in this light it sounds ridiculous that we should identify with what we do or what we have, but this is currently how the world goes round. Never forget who you truly are.

A Personal Experience

One day I decided to focus my meditation on the habit of attachment. So I held it there in my mind and watched. Gradually a trickle of insights turned into waves of realisations. One of those realisations hit me like a sledgehammer. Whatever I become attached to I lose my power to. And then I saw all the things that were draining my power. And then I saw that if I let go, I would get my power back. And that's when my self-respect began to return.

Journal Exercises

A. Origins of Thought

The root of all our actions and habits lies in our self identity. How we see ourselves is the seed of all our habits. To demonstrate this insight to yourself, try the following exercise (there is an example on the next page).

Step 1: Identify a sanskara (trait/tendency/habit) based on your professional identity (that is, the habit of identifying yourself with your profession/vocation/job).

Step 2: Write down one thought that comes from that sanskara.

Step 3: Was that thought a healthy one? (The chances are that it wasn't!)

Step 4: Change the unhealthy thought into a positive equivalent.

Here is a worked example to help you. Imagine I am a project manager in a company that provides training for people who work in the media.

Step 1: I haven't had a holiday for nearly five years because I worry about my position in the firm.
(*This is the sanskara of not doing something – in this case, not taking a holiday – because of fear or lack of trust, etc.*)

Step 2: Thought: "If I go to Corfu for three weeks with my family, I won't enjoy myself because I line manage a team of five and I am sure they won't be able to do their jobs properly without me."
(*Note the conditional 'if', the negative 'won'ts' and the 'without me' assumption that I am indispensable.*)

Step 3: No, the thought was not healthy – shows a sanskara of wanting to control, a sanskara of a lack of confidence/trust in others and a sanskara of arrogance that 'only I' know how to do the job.

Step 4: A positive equivalent: "I'm able to take a holiday in Corfu this year with my family because my team of five are smart enough to cope in my absence. Even if they have any problems in my absence, they can always contact me on my cell phone."
(*Here, I place trust in the team to get on with the job. I can still take a holiday and I'm only a phone call away in the event of a crisis.*)

In the example, the idea is implicit that if things go wrong while I am away, I am the one who will have to face the music. The result is that I postpone action (or procrastinate) due to a sanskara of fear.

The Journey Home

**Understanding and exploring the different
levels of consciousness**

Our original and natural awareness of ourselves as spiritual
beings has been replaced by the illusion that we are the bodies
we occupy. One of the many consequences of this unconscious
mistake is that we give almost all our time and attention to material
objects and processes. In our obsession with all things material,
including our own and others' physical bodies, we see and measure
others by their physical form. We compare our own shape with that
of others. Our success is measured by the quantity of our material
acquisitions. Doing has become much more important than being, as
we make the clock our master and speed our God. Then we try to
cram more activities into the space we call a day. It is all part and
parcel of identifying with our form and the things we do through our
form. We become trapped in the lowest form of consciousness - body
consciousness - and cannot see the trap. We lose ourselves in action
and become blind to the way we make everything seem urgent.

When we identify with our body, we create our ego – the false sense of self – and this is what gives rise to all forms of negative thinking and emotional pain. When we identify with the physical, we lose our sense of self in something that must change, decay and even be destroyed. When external objects and circumstances, including other people, mean more to us than we do to ourselves, we feel we have no control over our lives and are at the mercy of uncontrollable forces. This is what generates fear, tension, anxiety, worry and anger – the principal emotions which lie behind almost all physical disease. When we are mentally attached to something or someone, in such a way that we base our sense of happiness solely on the external, then mental/emotional pain arises if this 'attachment' is disturbed or even removed from our lives (either temporarily or permanently). We are even taught to invest our hopes and dreams in the lives of others and our entertainment industries rely on our living our lives through the fictional characters they create. As a consequence, both our potential and our aspirations remain unknown, any desire to be all that we can be is unfulfilled and we are no longer able to retain a healthy sense of self-esteem.

While the price we pay for our loss of soul-consciousness is some form of suffering, we can also use this suffering as our messenger and let it tell us that we are asleep again to our true spiritual nature. Pain, at any level, is simply a wake up call. However, instead of listening to the messenger, we frequently either send the messenger away (thereby denying that the problem exists) or we wallow in the pain (under the illusion that a bit of pain is good). In fact, we often convince ourselves that pain and suffering are inevitable and even necessary. We grow accustomed to the pain of fear and anxiety, and we see no harm in the occasional outburst of anger and rage. Such negative emotions become regular features on the landscape of daily living. If anyone suggests it would be better to remove them, we

resist the idea, as we cannot imagine life without our daily dose of negativity and the adrenaline that it produces. There is also the argument in some areas of psychology and self development that we should not suppress our emotions, that it is healthy to 'express' ourselves. This, however, only strengthens the sanskara/habit (see Lesson Four) of creating our negative emotions. The spiritual solution is to stop creating such emotions and to draw, from the core of our consciousness, the qualities of love, truth and peace and use these to create our thoughts and attitudes to the world around us. If we are to truly have an awareness of the original nature of the self, then it is not a question of suppression and/or expression – on the contrary, we focus on our natural positive qualities and simply don't give any space to the negative.

However, before we can do that there is one powerful truth we need to see and accept, which is the principle of self-responsibility.

Self-Responsibility

Changing the quality of our life experience means choosing the quality of our inner life. This begins by acknowledging and accepting that any pain or suffering is unnatural and that something has to be changed within our own consciousness. As with the physical body, where just being free from disease does not necessarily mean that we have reached a state of optimum health, so too the spirit within needs to be freed from the habit of tolerating even low levels of pain. However, we are often unable to change our habitual self-perception as victim because one of our deepest habits is to attribute our pain to someone else. We forget that no matter what is happening around us only we are responsible for our own thoughts and feelings. No-one can make us feel anything without our permission. An accurate knowledge and understanding of spirit reminds us that any pain or suffering is there because we have lost our true self-awareness. And yet, it's OK! Although the pain is not natural, it is part of the plan. It is the price we all pay for our spiritual amnesia, from falling asleep to who and what we are.

The road home and our true awakening begins with the acceptance that wherever we are is wherever we are meant to be at this particular moment in time, and whatever we are experiencing is whatever we are meant to be experiencing. Instead of trying to escape from a difficult situation, we need to understand that we are in the process of learning more about ourselves. Instead of attributing our mental or emotional discomfort to someone or some circumstance, which is really a form of disempowerment, we will benefit by acknowledging that we are fully responsible for whatever thoughts, feelings or emotions we have at this moment. This accepting of self-responsibility is the beginning of self-empowerment. If our experience is one of pain or discomfort, then it is a signal that we are not creating the highest quality of thoughts and feelings, or

we are not doing the right thing at the level of action. If we can be aware of the signal suffering brings, and value its message, we will then accept there is something we need to think, feel or do differently to free ourselves from a self-imposed prison.

While a caged bird's freedom lies outside the cage, our freedom awaits us within. We have an inner journey to make from body-consciousness to soul-consciousness, from dependency to independence, from fear to love, from being the slave of our senses to being the master of our senses. In meditation we sit in the driving seat of our conscious awareness, the fuel for our journey comes from the realisation and experience of the truth of who we are, and the direction is set at every moment as we 'consciously' decide where our attention and awareness go. This is the real work of self-mastery and the beginning of the journey home.

The metaphor of a journey is a good way to perceive our life, and
perhaps several lives. The journey is also defined by our day-to-day
relationships with other souls. With some, we form profoundly
strong bonds during a grand joint adventure, perhaps across several
births. Our relationships would be completely harmonious if only we
knew who we are and acted from that truth. In forgetting ourselves,
we complicate our relationships with the many masks we learn to
wear from a variety of motives, not least so that we may protect
ourselves from others whom we wrongly learn to perceive as
threatening. We forget that we cannot be threatened. Only what we
are attached to can be threatened; that is, our false self-images or
beliefs which form the basis of our ego. These masks are at the core
of the games we play in our interactions with family, friends,
colleagues and co-workers. Instead of being open and honest, loving
and kind, we build barriers and play evasive or confrontational
games, criticising and gossiping games – all signs that we are not
content within ourselves. They are symptoms of our own insecurity.
Our insecurity is a symptom of our spiritual amnesia.

The day-to-day work of awakening and self-transformation involves seeing ourselves playing these games, and freeing ourselves from thought and behaviour patterns we have created over time. Once again, meditation becomes a vital exercise of reflection, seeing and remembrance.

Only when we realise that we are responsible for any mental and emotional pain that we are experiencing will we be interested enough to take time out to **reflect**. Only when we reflect on our daily experience will we **see** the patterns (sanskaras) that are the cause of our discomfort. Only then can we break the patterns. The most effective way to break a pattern, from a purely spiritual point of view, is not to struggle with it, but simply see the pattern, remind ourselves of who we are as spirit, **remember** our self as soul, and to reconnect with our true peaceful, positive and loving nature. When we learn to **reflect,** without self-judgment, on our experience, we start to **see** the illusions that we have learned. These are the roots of the patterns of belief and thought which are causing our suffering.

Then, by consistently **remembering** who and what we are, through our meditation, we invoke the innate power of our peace, the power of our love and the power of truth. These innate powers then dissolve the old patterns which we now know were based on illusion and false belief.

Inwards and Upwards

While we do this inner work in the context of our 'horizontal' relationships (with others, nature and the physical environment), there is also a 'vertical' aspect to our journey which is equally important, our relationship with God. It is a journey only for the soul, and not the body, as we learn to move to higher levels of

consciousness through meditation and yoga. It is the 'journey home', a purely spiritual journey by which we return to our original, pure state of being, where we are completely free of the illusion that we are physical entities, where we are totally free of the noise of uncontrolled mental chatter and the emotional pain to which we have grown accustomed and, in some cases, addicted. While it is vital to restore authority over the faculties of our consciousness (see Lesson Four), equally important is the mastery of the three main levels of consciousness, sometimes referred to as the 'three worlds' – the physical world, the subtle world and the soul world.

Our spiritual journey home begins from where we find ourselves now, which, for most of us, is the physical or corporeal world.

The Physical World
The solid physical world of movement and sound

This is the world around us where we find the laws of science and the properties of matter in operation. Our physical environment is full of noise and constant movement as we play our various roles through our physical bodies on the stage of life. We express ourselves through our physical form and experience others through our physical senses. We relate directly to and interact with other souls as we exchange energy in all our relationships. But this is a limited world defined by the dimensions of time[13] and space. Almost all of us are now in this state of consciousness – aware only of the physical. It is not sleep, but compared to where we have come from it is a very sleepy state of awareness. Some souls have become so sleepy, so unaware, that they think this physical state of conscious awareness is all there is. The moment we identify with anything or anyone within this physical world, in that moment it is as if we are asleep. As we have seen, the recurring theme of this course is that meditation is the method to break the habit of identifying with the physical, awaken ourselves and learn to be who we truly are. Only then can we begin to allow that true sense of self to influence our thoughts and actions.

One of the fruits of the practice of meditation, along with detachment from physical objects and surroundings, is the development of an awareness of 'the subtle', of a dimension beyond our understanding of the purely physical.

The Subtle World
The mental world of movement but no sound

This is an intermediate dimension of purity and light, beyond the physical world. It is a place (or state of consciousness) where we are able to experience our subtle, light form, which is pure, carefree and light in character. We can reach this subtle region through our thoughts and, although we may not literally experience light, there is

an experience of being detached from the physical body and an awareness of subtle vibrations.

In meditation, we go beyond the consciousness of the physical body and the awareness of the physical world. With pure, spiritual thoughts, the soul can change the nature of the energy it gives out (vibration) and move easily into this level.

This subtle region of pure, white light is like a cocoon of light around the physical world. In this state, communication requires no sound, only vibration. Just as we are able to walk into a room and experience something in the atmosphere, so too we are able to feel the pure, positive energy of ourselves and other souls when we are in this subtle state of consciousness.

Beyond this subtle region of pure consciousness lies our true home, our original dwelling place and now the destination of our spiritual journey. It is not so much a place as a state of consciousness that takes us beyond both the physical and subtle worlds (states of consciousness).

The Soul World
The incorporeal world of no movement and no sound

Beyond the physical world of constant change, noise and movement, beyond the subtle region of pure thought, there is a dimension of complete silence and perfect stillness where time has no reference. This is the world of the soul or the home of all souls. Here the soul is in its inactive state. It is not doing, it is being. The soul is completely detached and separate from the body, and exists in its original state in the form of a spark of spiritual energy. It is from here, and from this state of being, that we all come and we will all eventually return.

To perceive this dimension and experience this pure state of soul-consciousness, imagine for a moment that you, the soul, the conscious point of spiritual light, have moved outside your body. You no longer have your senses. You cannot see, hear, touch, taste or feel. You can't speak or communicate. You just are. You have no

need to think about anything, no decisions to make. You are not asleep or non-existent, you are simply totally absorbed in your own being.[14]

This is the experience in the soul world, a dimension of complete silence and stillness. You are light, suspended in light, beyond the boundaries of the physical universe, beyond the boundaries of your own thoughts. When we are in this original state of being, we are like seeds, dormant, but with the complete future plan of our life's expression within is merged within us like a blueprint.

It is also in this dimension or state of consciousness that we encounter the Source, the One who has been called by many names down through the ages (God, Allah, Ishwar, Jehovah, etc.), but always remembered as light. This is the Supreme Soul, the spiritual Parent of all souls, who exists eternally in this dimension of spirit or the Soul World. It is in this seed state of being, in the presence of the Source of spirit, that we are spiritually refreshed in preparation for our emergence into the world of action and interaction with others. It is in this state that we are spiritually recharged. Like a solar panel absorbing the light of the sun we absorb that light of the spiritual sun. The Creator heals and renews the soul. This is re-creation.

Before exploring the identity, nature and role of the Creator, it is useful at this stage to consolidate and strengthen our meditation experience. It is through meditation that we can learn to create the states of consciousness which enable us to move easily between all three worlds. Use the following meditations to take you into your highest state of consciousness – the state of complete silence, where you, the soul, are truly like a tiny seed, with everything merged within you.

Making the Journey Home through Meditation

First Step - Leaving the physical world

As we saw in Lesson Four, one of the most effective inner skills that meditation helps us to develop is to disengage, stand back and become a detached observer. This is not a form of escape but a way of learning to use our energy in a more efficient way. Being a detached observer allows us to witness life around us without losing or wasting our mental energy on issues and events over which we have no control and that are not important to us. Being a detached observer also allows us to see a more complete picture of what is happening, whether it is an international scene or a domestic situation. It is also the basis of self-control, allowing us to keep unhelpful emotions in check and to bring forth all that is good within ourselves. Being detached from the world around us while observing without judgment or resistance to anyone or anything allows us to return to our soul-conscious state easily and quickly.

Meditation 6 – The Detached Observer

The next time you find yourself in an intense interaction, feed the following thoughts into your mind, pausing momentarily between thoughts, allowing yourself enough time to slow down and focus.

I am soul and at peace with myself and the world around me...
This scene is one of thousands in which I choose to play a role...
I disengage for a moment from what is happening around me...
Mentally, I take a step back and just watch dispassionately what is happening...
I make no judgments or assessment – I just observe...
As I observe, I see that soul is playing their own unique role, according to their understanding...
My acceptance of each one is total and unconditional...
As I watch, I also become aware of my patience in allowing this scene to evolve naturally...
I wait for an invitation to participate – it always comes eventually...
I have no personal agenda ... no desires...
I am happy to contribute towards achieving the most positive and

effective outcome...

In the meantime I watch, while remaining at peace within myself...

I share the vibration of that peace with all around me in the knowledge that this is the most valuable contribution that I can make...

I realise that simply by observing peacefully I am participating positively in this scene...

To maintain my peace I remain the detached observer.

If you dedicate time to consciously practise the above meditation 'in action', you will eventually find that you move into this state of being naturally and easily. You are not avoiding or escaping from life or the reality of the world around you. Instead, you are learning to control your awareness and involvement, disengage at will, be more sensitive to all that is happening around you and give yourself the time and the space to measure your response. You are also developing a deeper awareness of the subtle energies at play within yourself and others. You are being 'soul-conscious' while being aware of the drama of life, unfolding as it should, around you.

Second Step - Moving into a more subtle world

As well as our physical form, we each have a form of light – a subtle body. Sometimes referred to as the aura, it can be 'seen' by some sensitive souls, but most of us only become aware of it through the vibrations of others. The purity of our light form is dependent on the purity of our thought or mental vibrations. The daily practice of Raja Yoga Meditation is the main method by which we purify our thoughts and raise the quality of our vibrations. In this way we can move into, and be more aware of, the 'subtle region'. This will also help us increase our sensitivity to all the subtleties of daily life.

Meditation 7 – Being Light

Here are some thoughts for your meditation to take you into the a subtle world of pure light. Take your time and allow yourself to live each thought.

I am now detached from the physical world around me and simply observing...
I become aware of the constant activity in my mind...
I consciously create only the purest thoughts...
I am a subtle being of pure spiritual light...
I become aware of my subtle body of pure, white light surrounding my physical form...
In my body of light, I consciously stand up and step away from my physical form, which remains seated...
The light of my subtle form is like that of an angel – radiating out into the world...
Each thought is like a fine strand of silk, shimmering into the world around me...
Each strand carries a vibration of pure peace, a gift to any being that it may touch...
Each strand is a thought so subtle, so fine, yet so powerful, so pure...
In this pure awareness of myself in my form of light, I realise that the greatest gifts I can share with those around me are
the light of love, the light of peace, the light of truth.

As you practise the art of being aware of your subtle body, you will begin to sense how you can have a positive effect on others simply radiating good wishes, pure thoughts and pure feelings. You become aware of how the atmosphere in a room or between people can be enhanced simply by your moving into this subtle state of pure being, with the intention of contributing the highest possible vibrations towards the people and the process around you.

Third Step - Arriving in the soul world

Our original dwelling place is a dimension of soft, golden light, a place of absolute silence and stillness. This is where we used 'to be' in our original form of a point of radiant light. In this dimension, everything is merged within our consciousness. Like a seed, we are life waiting to happen. We are poised to emerge and express our unique beauty through the form of a body. Through our physical form we will be able to radiate the fragrance of our spiritual qualities. For the soul, this original, seed-like state is like being at home. The deepest form of meditation is one in which we return to this dimension of soft, golden light. It is a state of being which we can practise experiencing while we are still in our bodies.

Meditation 8 – Going Home

As your meditation deepens with practice, you will find yourself able to go beyond the awareness of the world around you, to go beyond your own thoughts and feelings and to arrive in a state of deep inner silence. Here are some thoughts for a meditation which will take you to this state of consciousness. In this meditation you are using thought to go beyond thought.

I am a spirit being who has travelled far and I am about to make the final journey home...
I willingly release my awareness of the physical world around me, and of my physical body, for a moment...

I centre my awareness of myself in the middle of my forehead just above and behind the eyes...
I become aware of my 'subtle' body of light...
I feel myself moving easily upwards, away from the physical space I have been sitting in, and out into the world...
I continue to rise high above into the vastness of the sky...

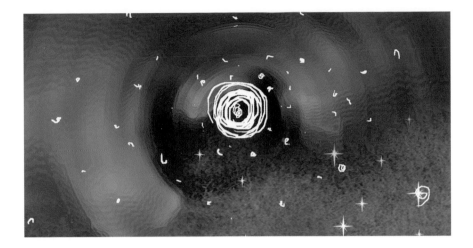

I enjoy the feeling of the freedom of a bird on the wing...

Ahead I can see space in all its majesty approaching

In a split second, my subtle body collapses into a tiny point of shimmering white light...

Like a comet I race past a thousand galaxies...

Almost as quickly, I slow down and I enter an area of warm, golden light...

Like a quilt of the softest down, it enfolds me...

I know this place so well...

I have reached the silent world that is my eternal home...

I am completely still...

There is no movement, no sound, no thought, no feeling...

Yet I am aware...

I am aware of the deepest peace...

I am aware of the most profound silence...

Like a seed in its original state, I am the soul in my original state...

Everything I have ever known and done is merged within...

I am aware of the presence of another who has only benevolence in His heart for me...

I decide to stay and enjoy this eternal moment of the deepest peace in this silent, loving reunion, in the comfort of my original home.

Within each one of us is the experience of each of these states of being, or levels of consciousness. Even in the physical world any journey begins from home and eventually brings us back home – so it is with the journey of spirit. Our spiritual home, the home of all souls, is the soul world, a dimension beyond time and space, where we remain silent and in the company of our spiritual Parent. The purpose of leaving our home, the reason for our journey into the physical world of time and space, is simply to live and know life. It is to know ourselves, to express the inner beauty of our unique nature, and to experience the nature and the beauty of others. To do this we need to be in a physical form, with our five senses and together with others in the same time dimension. Here, we are together, expressing ourselves and being creative – creating our own lives, as well as working with, caring for, helping and appreciating others in their creation. In the co-creation of our grand adventure together, we each have the opportunity to enrich and be enriched. When we began the journey the predominant energy was pure love. In our journey through time and our gradual loss of true self-awareness, love has turned to fear. Which is why we now experience so much division and conflict at all levels of our modern societies.

When we lose awareness of this purpose or reason for being here, when we think that 'here' is all there is and when we place the material above the spiritual on our scale of values (the outer before the inner), our life becomes much less playful and joyful. Life becomes quite serious and we turn our relationships into a business. "I'll give, if you give. I'll love you, if you'll love me." We become dependent and begin to fear that we will not be loved, so our love turns to fear. Unhappiness is a natural consequence of making life serious in this way. Unhappiness trickles down from the spiritual, to the mental, to the emotional, and ultimately affects our physical well-being. But deep down inside, there is always a voice calling us back, reminding us, whispering its truth to us. While we have succumbed to the illusion that we are only physical beings and that life is survival of the fittest, this quiet inner voice gently reminds us that this is not who we are, this is not why we are here. You are not

what you see in the bathroom mirror and you did not come here to be in perpetual anxiety. This is who you are, this is why you came – come home, be yourself, be aware and be free again. Be love, give love and be loved again.

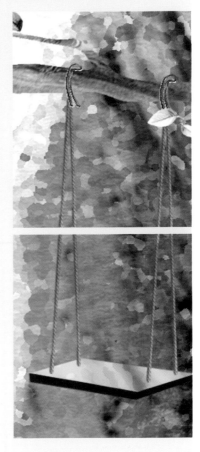

The call of our spiritual home and our original state of consciousness is always there, just as much as the memory of home from our childhood experiences in this birth is always within our consciousness. Sometimes we go back to visit the place where we were brought up and played as children. We re-experience the special feelings and significant moments. For every soul on Earth there is a spiritual home that calls us. For every soul on Earth there was a spiritual childhood filled with innocence, joy and blissful happiness. It is a place of pure peace and contentment, a dimension beyond time and space. It calls us and it beckons us to return. It is a journey of no distance and it takes only one second!

Frequently Asked Questions

Q.   *Do we go home when we die?*

A.   When we understand and experience ourselves as souls, as imperishable, eternal beings, we realise that death is only a physical phenomenon. At the death of the body, the soul makes the transition into another physical costume and a new chapter in the adventure of life begins. Depending on the soul's karma (the record of action through the body), this is likely to be somewhere in the orbit of the souls with whom it has been close in previous births. As we will see in later lessons, the soul only leaves the home once in a unique, personal journey, which is not linear but cyclical. This pattern can be likened to actors who leave home to go to the theatre to play their parts. They change costumes between scenes – they don't return home at the end of each act or scene, they return home when the play is finished, only to return the next day to repeat their part. Each birth that we take can be likened to a new act of the play with many scenes. It is a new chapter in the book of our journey into and through this world – more on that in a later lesson.

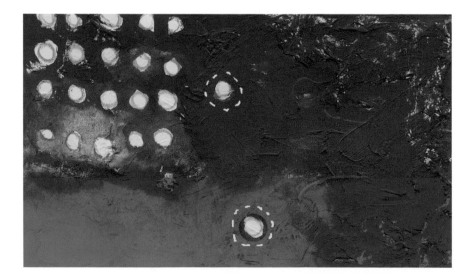

Q.   *When you say the soul falls asleep, what do you mean exactly?*

A.   Even though we are awake and aware of the world around us it is as if we are asleep and unable to see the world as it truly is, unable to see others as they truly are and unable to see events in their true light. The word 'see' really means perceive.

Our intellect perceives the world and interprets the world according to what it has learned to believe and according to past experiences. If we have learned to believe we are bodies and not souls, if we have learned to believe that our emotions are created by others, if we have learned to believe that the world is evolving in a positive and progressive way, these beliefs will influence our perception and interpretation of other people, situations and world events in a certain way.

Our thoughts, emotions and behaviours follow accordingly. Each of these beliefs is wrong - but don't believe me! In essence we are asleep to the truth, so we sleepwalk our way through life and don't even know it. As a consequence of wrong beliefs, we will create pain or suffering in some form, at some inner level, but we will tolerate the pain in the belief that it

must be normal. It is only when the suffering becomes so great that we acknowledge we have to do something about it. And here you are, doing something about it by reading this book on meditation to see if it will help you understand your pain and transform your pain. Which it will. Just reading the book won't change much beyond your understanding. Only the practice of meditation and the inner study of the simple truths you find here will eventually heal your pain (spiritual, mental and emotional). Meditation and ongoing spiritual study help you to awaken and stay awake to the deeper realities of life around you and to the eternal truths which already lie within you.

Q.   *Surely if I make this 'journey home' will I not have to leave my body and therefore die?*

A.   This is a journey through levels of consciousness. You don't leave your body, you simple refine your awareness and with each refinement you 'go beyond' the awareness of the last level. For example, right now you are aware of the physical world around you, the room, perhaps an itch in your leg and of course you are aware of this book. Stop now and meditate for a moment, withdraw your attention and then your awareness from everything outside and around you. Be aware only of your inner world, your thoughts and feelings in this moment now. Then go beyond the awareness of your thoughts and feelings. Be aware of yourself like a seed, everything totally merged within. You are completely still yet fully aware of yourself. Notice the power of being in this awareness, not power over anything, simply the power of being, the power of the self. The journey home is not to a place in the physical sense, but to a level of awareness or state of consciousness which can be likened to the original state from which you began your journey into this corporeal world.

Q.   *Isn't refining our state of conscious awareness and 'going beyond' just another escape from the 'real world'?*

A.   Actually the purpose of this journey is three-fold. First it is an essential inner exercise in which we re-learn to choose and control our state of consciousness. Secondly it is an inner process which can only happen when we learn to detach, which means letting go of our accumulated negative habits of thought, negative emotional tendencies and negative memories.   Which is why the journey home could also be described as the only journey where you are guaranteed to lose your baggage! Third, it is an inner process of renewal and empowerment. As you master the process of moving through these states of consciousness you regain your spiritual power that was previously trapped or suppressed by the illusions based on identification only with form. The journey home is not an escape from reality but a return to a higher reality. Unreality for the soul is the belief that the physical world is all there is and that happiness always requires some physically stimulated experience.

Q.   *So if the higher reality lies beyond this world does that mean we may as well give up on this world and just 'go home'?*
A.   Although that may be an appealing idea to some, it is not possible until the right moment. In truth it is our karma which keeps us here, which is another way of saying, keeps us aware of the physical world of form. Our karma is the creation of these inner negativities mentioned above. The clearing of our karma comes with the practice of raising our consciousness, through meditation, back to its original and highest consciousness (see Lesson Seven).

A Personal Experience

It was the most powerful meditation I had ever had, almost without trying. Almost immediately after I sat down I felt a powerful urge to go deep inside. And then I felt a pull to what I can only describe as beyond! I completely lost awareness of everything around me and I was in another world. I can only describe it as light, soft, warm golden light. And I felt a presence of another Being. I knew who it was. I recognised Him instantly and I knew He recognised me. I could feel His love. At one point it was so powerful it was almost overwhelming, I have never known such a feeling before. I was aware of one tiny thought which crossed my mind, to turn the volume down, and immediately He did, and I instantly regretted the thought and I could swear He smiled – but of course there was no face. But then something pulled me out and back into the room. I was absolutely stunned by the depth of the experience – I still remember it to this day. It took me ages to be fully aware of the physical. I kept wanting to go back.

Questions to - meditation@bkpublications.com

Journal Exercise

A. Seeing Beauty

For the next seven days, focus on something that you consider to be beautiful and/or inspiring. Don't get lost in it but consciously identify what are the attributes or characteristics that you consider beautiful or inspirational. Note down what you see below.

Day	Beautiful	Inspiring
1		
2		
3		
4		
5		
6		
7		

B. Visiting your Life

Spend your next free weekend imagining that you are a tourist or guest who has come to observe your own own life. Tourists and guests usually appreciate the things that we usually take for granted and they also notice details that we tend to ignore. Make a note below of your experience, identifying areas of your life that you realise that you have been neglecting recently.

C. Beyond Your Senses

Find yourself a quiet space and a time when you know there won't be any interruptions. Sit down quietly and concentrate on being observant of your senses. What can you see, hear, smell, feel and taste? Now, one by one, withdraw your consciousness from these senses. Imagine that you are in a world with no colour, no sound, no fragrances, no sensations and no tastes. Do this exercise slowly: firstly, with conscious awareness and then detaching yourself and finally bringing your awareness back to your senses. Record your experience below.

D. Out of this World

Create a short story entitled *Rebecca visits the Worlds of Solid, Subtle and Sublime*. Describe Rebecca's adventure as she moves from one world to another and what she discovers in each world.

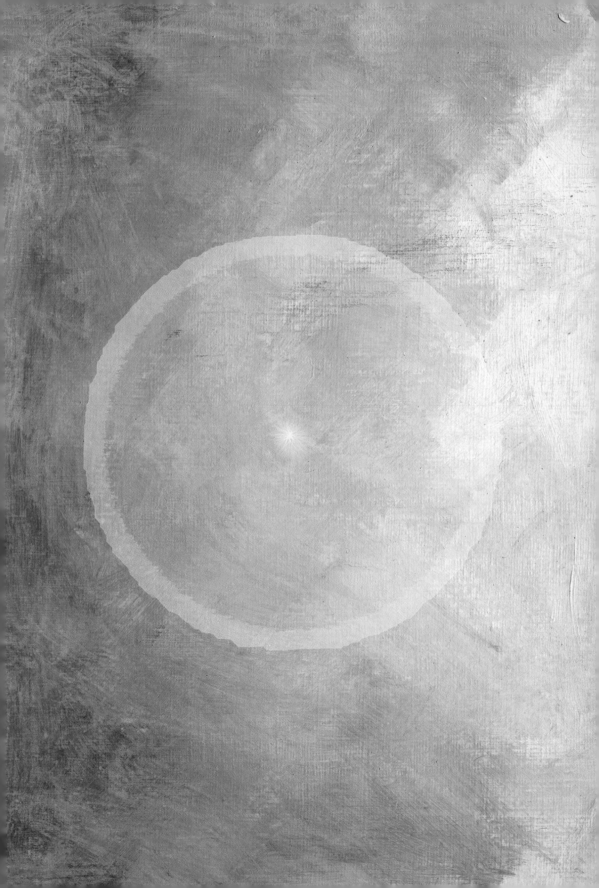

Reunion with the Source

Restoring and cultivating our silent, loving
relationship with God

Far beyond this world of time, matter and action, there is a
world of complete silence and stillness. There is no sound, no
movement, no hands of time directing existence; it cannot be called
a place in the normally accepted way that we think of a physical
place or space, and yet it is from this dimension that the soul comes.
This is our spiritual home. This is the world of eternity; silent and
unchanging. In the last meditation of Lesson Five, we used the
power of our thoughts to 'travel' to this silent dimension of light.

Residing permanently in this world beyond time and space is a point
of constant energy, an eternally bodiless, pure Being, remembered by
many as God. This point of pure, benevolent, all-knowing energy is
the spiritual Parent of all souls. This is the One who is referred to in
almost every religious and spiritual tradition and remembered as a
radiant light, a source of pure, unconditional love.

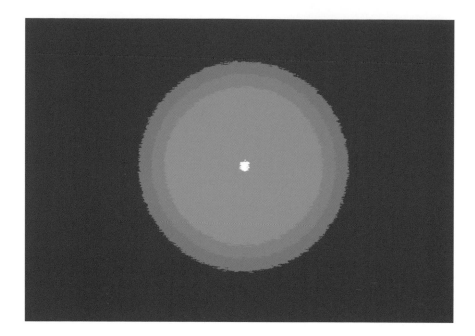

Living in this soundless, peaceful dimension of light and absolute
stillness, the Supreme Soul is the only being who is beyond the
influence of the change and decay to which we are all subject here on
Earth. Beyond our world of matter and forever incorporeal, God
does not enter this world of time and space, of movement and sound,
except at the moment when our collective negativity reaches its
extreme and we invoke His presence. As the volume of our painful
cries becomes louder (mentally and emotionally), He responds to our
call and donates His life force, the divine energy of His being, to
restore humanity and nature to its original state of purity and order.
If we understand the state of the world at this moment to be at its
most chaotic and see that the external chaos of our global
communities has its roots in the internal chaos of the human soul, it
becomes easier to understand that the restoration of order and
harmony in the world must begin within the soul. This is God's role
– to restore the peace and harmony in the world by restoring the
peace and purity of the human soul.

The Universal Search

Throughout history, human beings have desired and searched for two things, happiness and a perfect relationship. There is an old truth, *"You cannot search for what you have not already had or known."* In other words, our search is motivated by a deep subconscious memory of the original, perfect and eternal relationship with our Friend, Guide and Parent, the One remembered as God, Allah, Ishwar, Jehovah, etc. It is only when our relationship with this Being is restored that we can experience true happiness or bliss. Bliss is the deepest spiritual happiness we can experience. It is experienced only when we are free of all attachment, when we no longer misidentify with anything physical and when our state of being is not dependent on anything or anyone.

At its highest level, our relationship with God is pure and non-dependent, and therefore blissful. Deep within the soul, there is a memory of the bliss of this perfect communion and it is the deepest motivation in our search for the perfect relationship, for the perfect happiness. However, instead of seeking at the level of spirit, we seek at the level of mind (personality) and body. We search in those around us for the perfect partner – our soul mate – little realising that our true soul mate, our true beloved, is the One with whom we have an eternal relationship, the One with whom we have the deepest bond.

Knowing and Understanding God

To rediscover and restore our conscious awareness of our relationship with God, a belief in God is not initially essential; in fact, it can be an obstacle. If we have already developed or learnt certain concepts about God, these concepts may themselves be a barrier. An openness to the idea that there may be a greater source of spiritual energy than ourselves is of most use. Only if our minds are open, can we be ready to communicate personally and directly.

What tends to keep our minds closed to God are either the beliefs we have learnt or inherited from our education and our culture or the trust we have invested in those who themselves have a closed mind and are unaware of it. It is at this point that we find the divergence of religion and spirituality. Religion would have us 'believe' there is a God, and often a belief that it is not possible to know God, directly or indirectly, or to even approach God. Or, in the case of Buddhism, there is often the belief that there is no God at all. Each religion's beliefs can be a threat to the others, especially when the name of God is recruited to support their beliefs and actions. Spirituality, on the other hand, encourages us to leave all limited beliefs behind and be both humble and open to the possibility of the presence of God in our life. Hence the value of personal experience before a learned or inherited belief. Hence the essential need for a method such as meditation to make the bridge from belief to direct experience. In meditation the soul/self releases any false attachments, including learned beliefs, and opens to receive and directly experience the light of the Source.

Religion also tends to encourage us to have faith, to pray and perhaps beg to a being in whose face, it is often said, we are not worthy to look. On the other hand, spirituality would have us believe nothing blindly and never diminishes our own innate but now suppressed divinity. The spiritual approach to God is one of cultivating a relationship that is as real, direct and as dynamic as we might have with a member of our family. It means that personal experience is the only real validation of God's presence in our life. While religion would tend to encourage strict adherence to a set of recorded and institutionalised beliefs, spirituality would say, "You must not believe me when I say it is snowing outside – go and see for yourself. Here, I'll show you the way, but you must go and see and touch the snow for yourself." Spirituality would not encourage blind faith in an historical set of other people's beliefs, but would encourage the cultivation of an enlightened faith based on own personal experience. God does not want to be worshiped, only to see His loved ones awakened from their self-imposed spiritual slumber!

The religious mind-set is sometimes threatened by this approach and sometimes calls it self-indulgent and self-absorbed. Spirituality calls it the awakening of the self/soul to an awareness of its true form and nature, while reminding us that everything and everyone are interconnected. While we are all unique and have individual characteristics, we are also members of one spiritual family. If we are each awakened enough to restore our personal link with the Source, with God, then that in itself will benefit all others around us. Seen in this way the enlightenment of the self becomes a spiritual service to others.

This does not mean that the religious person is not spiritual. Many are naturally spiritual and carry a healthy scepticism about organised belief systems and the institutions which are built around them. They are often drawn to the universal truths found at an intellectual level in all religious philosophies. But an intellectual understanding is not enough, as the mystics and the saints have reminded us through the ages. Their testimonies, which contain direct experiences of a transcendent Being, stand out to remind us that God can never easily be subject to scientific scrutiny, but rather will be found in the personal, subjective experience of spiritual communication. For this reason there is always an emphasis on the practice of meditation/contemplation and the purification of spirit.

Ideas, concepts and beliefs about God, or others' experiences of God, are not enough for us to connect and communicate personally with the Source. It would be likened to thinking that the flower in a locked cupboard below the stairs is able to receive the light and warmth of the sun. We would be attempting to communicate with a concept and not a real Being. Neither is ritual or worship sufficient to make deep contact and draw spiritual power from the Source of all power. In the process of the blind reverence found in devotion and worship, the absence of self-recognition is the barrier to a deep heart-to-heart connection. While we would personally benefit from the ability to demonstrate love towards the object of our devotion (to generate and express love is to experience love), we are not able to see and correct our own personal faults and weaknesses, and therefore not humble enough to be open to the healing and purifying energy of the Sun of spirit. It could be likened to a patient forgetting why they went to see the doctor, worshipping the doctor for his/her wonderful abilities to heal, but not realising that they need treatment themselves, nor recognising the role they need to play in their own healing.

The word 'God' can also be difficult. It can trigger the emergence of much subconscious baggage – for example, killing in the name of God, punishment for sin, the threat of being converted or blind obedience to a cult or sect.

Depending on our conditioning, any or all of these ideas and images can invade our minds, causing us to step back into scepticism and perhaps atheism. Each of these factors, plus the current, dark, chaotic state of our world which frequently seems bereft of any real meaning, all give rise to the convenient idea that, at worst, God is dead, at best, God is absent. This is appealing to some because it means that we can avoid making the effort to reconnect and re-establish our personal relationship with our spiritual Parent. Instead, we invent easier gods to whom we can express our devotional tendencies. Sport, entertainment, literature, the gurus of enlightenment are all areas where we find or invent a god (or two) to worship and mentally commune with. Disappointment and disillusion are always the eventual outcomes of creating gods in our ungodly, mundane world. None can deliver the purity, truth, love and light which are both the yearning of the heart and now our greatest need. Once again, all these longings and behaviours demonstrate that we have a deep memory of a very elevated Being who means so much to us and in whom we want to invest our love and trust. We cannot search for what we do not already know. God is not dead, but simply lost to our awareness. He is waiting for us to awaken to who we really are as spirit and for us to restore the humility we require to keep our mind and heart open to receiving His presence in our lives. For many of us, this only happens when we reach the lowest point in our journey and the inner darkness, induced by our own ego, is so painful that we say, "Enough is enough. I give up. Help me!" Locked into what is often called the 'dark night of the soul', sapped of energy and ready to give up the struggle to sustain our own illusions, we surrender to the need for help. So often this deep despair, encountered on the soul's journey, precedes the beginning of true enlightenment and the re-entry of God into our lives. Perhaps you have touched that point, perhaps you recognise that moment or perhaps you are open to that possibility.

Yet, if we want to have contact with the Supreme Being, there are certain things that we must know:

•   firstly, the form of the Supreme, so that we will be able to have accurate recognition.
•   secondly, we need to know what 'language' to use so that there can be communication.
•   thirdly, we need to know where we will meet.

Just as we have a very precise understanding of the form of the soul (self), so we also require a very precise notion of the form of the Supreme. In fact, His form is identical to that of the human soul; a point source of consciousness, a spark of light energy. When we use the word 'He', this is not to imply that the Supreme Soul is male. The soul itself has no gender; it is only the body which has gender. Whereas the human soul animates a physical body and thereby acquires gender, the Supreme Soul never has a body of His own and is, therefore, neither male nor female, yet the qualities of the

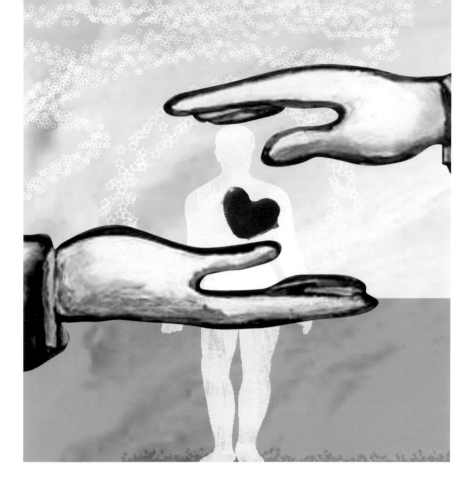

masculine and the feminine are present within Him. God never animates a physical form. He does not take human birth so, unlike us, He never loses awareness of who He is or His original attributes. He remains eternally pure, peaceful, full of love, blissful and powerful, and radiates the energy of those spiritual qualities at every moment.

However, when we lose our self-awareness, our consciousness is overshadowed by our mistaken identification with our physical form. We not only find our spiritual power diminished, but we find it difficult to receive the pure spiritual vibrations which emanate from Him. We cannot attune to receiving the pure light of the spiritual Sun when we are body-conscious. When the flower awakens in the morning it neither spends time admiring itself in a mirror, nor does it

look around and compare itself to others - two of our strongest
tendencies in a world obsessed with form. The flower immediately
turns to face the sun and opens itself to receive the light and warmth
that it needs in order to grow and be all that it can be. Similarly we
are in need of the light of truth and the warmth of pure love so that
our illusions can be dispelled and our broken hearts can be healed.
Unfortunately the sun in the morning sky cannot do this for us. This
spiritual quality of light and love comes from only one being, the
Sun of spirit, the Source. God is the one who loves, without
condition, every single being, regardless of their history, regardless of
who we think we are! As children of our spiritual parent, it is His
guiding light that we need to free us from delusion and confusion.
As our Mother, it is Her pure love that we need to restore the purity
of our heart and our ability to nourish the spirit of others.
Meditation and yoga are our methods to face and open ourselves to
the One who donates His power to restore the soul to its original,
pure and loving form.

To prepare ourselves for this connection and communion we first
need to ensure that we have the correct state of consciousness. In
meditation, we release our awareness of worldly distractions, turn

our attention within and become soul-conscious. Once we
have realised our inner peace, we can turn our attention
towards the Source and open ourselves to an intimate
exchange of the subtlest of energies, the pure light of love.
We will know that we have achieved union when our
silent, loving thoughts are returned by waves of love
penetrating our being, in the same way that the sun's warmth
penetrates our skin. We will be aware of the most subtle, powerful
Being, shining benevolence across our spiritual path, in rays of
light. It is these rays of light which purify and heal the
memories of wrong actions and thoughts which have left their
scars on the soul. They lift any heaviness and restore our

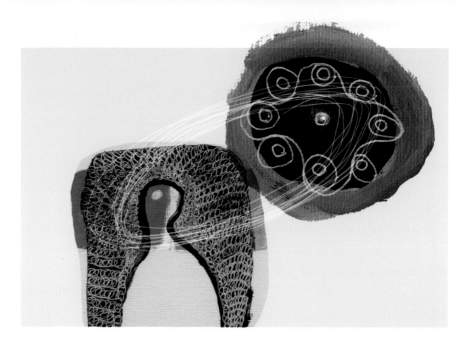

awareness of who we are and of our beauty within. These rays are also like seeds, planted in the soul, which burst forth in our intellects, often unexpectedly, to empower us and lighten our way in a world of many falsehoods. They serve to remind us that we have achieved yoga (union) and that we are now living in the light of our Parent, Friend and Guide, the Source of love, truth and power.

A true and healthy human relationship is built, sustained and matured in the exchanges of open, honest and intimate communication. Our relationship with God is no different, only that it is silent. The vibrations of our thoughts and feelings reach and touch the light that is the Source and are then reflected back with love and power. Ultimately, the meeting is a silent communion, free of the noise of thought, and there is an awareness of the presence of the Beloved in our life. The sense of relationship becomes just as real as a physical parent or friend. He is there in one second, available at any and every moment, not to deal with the mundane or to help out in emergencies, but to respond to our open and honest heart, and to use us, if we make ourselves available, so that others may be touched and awakened by His light and love.

Meditation 9 – Relationship with God

We each have a personal relationship with our spiritual Parent and meditation and yoga are the methods for reconnecting and cultivating that relationship. The key is communication with Him. This can be in thoughts, in silence or even writing a letter which sends the vibrations of an open and honest heart to the One who waits to re-enter our heart. The following thoughts may give some guidance. Eventually it is best if you can create your own thoughts.

Sitting quietly, my body is comfortable and relaxed...
I remind myself that I am an eternal being of light – a soul...
Even my relationship with my own body exists only for a short space of time...
I existed before this body and will continue to exist long after it perishes...
I can distance myself from the consciousness of my body...
When I do, I also realise that human relationships are truly fragile ....momentary...they ebb and flow...
One moment I have contact with an individual and the next moment it changes...
The only perpetual relationship that I have with every human being is that of brotherhood...[15]
I consciously move away from this sphere of influence of human beings, so I can explore the reality of my eternal connection with One – with the Supreme...
With one powerful thought I move my awareness away from this solid physical world and step back into the home of light, into the land of silence...
In this dimension of light, I become aware of the presence of a radiant Being of light...
As I allow myself to be touched and enfolded by that light I feel the purest love of the benevolent One

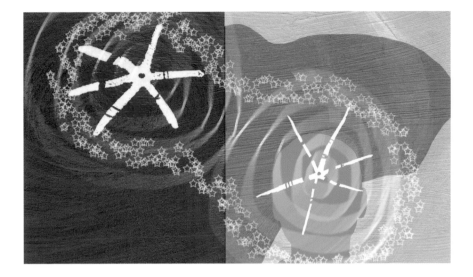

penetrating my heart...

I feel I am meeting my oldest and dearest friend after many years apart...

The joy of being together again is the sweetest feeling...

I can feel God's love and light flowing directly into my being...

Dispelling all darkness within my consciousness...

As a mother She holds me and comforts me and reassures me...

I feel Her love nurturing me and filling me with power...

I feel God's love as the love of complete acceptance, the true love of the parent for I the child...

I feel like a child again...Gods child again...

All doubt and all fear dissolves in Her presence...

I am not afraid of God...

I feel the sweetness and mercy of God's love pulling me towards itself...

As my Father he respects me without condition, without judgement...

As my eternal Friend I open my heart wide and tell Him everything...

In the sweet silence of this loving encounter, we are separate and yet one, different and yet so alike, silent and yet our communion is complete. ✳

Frequently Asked Questions

Q. *How can I restore and rebuild my relationship with God?*

A. Sometimes, in order to get where we need to go, we need to let go and to trust the process. We need to move from resistance to acceptance, even if it's only to experiment with new possibilities. Here are seven ways to overcome any resistance you may have at this moment to restoring and rebuilding your personal relationship with God.

1. Accept that the soul and the Supreme Soul are separate beings with the same form, radiant points of spiritual energy, infinitely small in size but infinitely vast in capacity.

2. Accept that it does not take many lives to find and reinvigorate our connection with the Supreme – only one second, one thought.

3. Accept that God does not require worship or blind devotion.

4. Accept that He is a loving God, a Parent who does not inflict pain or punishment but who only wants the best for His children – a compassionate and understanding God who knows why we fall asleep to our true awareness and create pain for ourselves.

5. Accept that the restoration of the loving link with God requires the suspension of our attachment to the material world of objects, ideas and people.

6. Accept that we must play our part in building our relationship with the Creator and that, like any relationship, it takes a little time to develop.

7. Accept that God is not present in the material world, He is not omnipresent. He is a very real, individual and unique Being.

Q.   *Many spiritual philosophies believe that God is everywhere. So, why do you say that He is not omnipresent?*

A.   It is not possible for God to be omnipresent – that is, in every person and every animal and the elements of nature. We were originally divine beings (with qualities like God) and that divine likeness is still within each soul. If God were within us we would not, as individuals, have free will. If God were omnipresent it would mean that God hates and God kills, and that God searches for and worships Himself, thereby saying that God is less than perfect and in ignorance. When we say God is in each of us and in nature, it is also a convenient way for us to avoid making the effort to change and improve ourselves. It is our way of avoiding the effort of playing our part in a real and dynamic relationship.

Q.   *Why does God punish innocent people?*

A.   He doesn't punish anyone. We punish ourselves as a result of wrong thinking and wrong action. Our conscience knows naturally what is right and wrong. When we act against the truth, some form of pain is our inevitable punishment (see Lesson Seven on Karma). All religious and spiritual thinkers agree that one part of a definition of God is that He is a perfect Being. If He is perfect, then it would be impossible for Him to carry out any action that could bring sorrow or suffering to any soul. As we have seen, ego is the root of all our suffering. Ego happens when we lose awareness of our true self and identify with something that we are not. All our punishments are therefore self-created, the result of our spiritual amnesia. All pain and suffering are therefore a wake up call!

Q.   *You talk about God being our Mother and Father – isn't this rather a difficult idea to accept?*

A.   God is not just a point. He is not just energy. God is a living Being and what is conscious and living has personality. Personality includes the capacity to create feelings, form relationships and to play a role in the drama of life. The two key relationships that God has with His creation are as the eternal Mother and Father. In these relationships are the combined masculine and feminine qualities which give life and sustenance. The eternal Father, out of His love, creates new life. He has the power to renew and reorder the universe. Through truth, He establishes harmony and well-being. Like the physical sun, the masculine principle is still, fixed, full of power radiating the light that transforms and recreates life. As the eternal Mother, God cares for and patiently nourishes the children with encouragement and selfless love. Like the physical Earth, the eternal feminine is ever giving, renewing and nurturing. Through the daily practice of meditation and yoga, you will gradually experience the healing, nurturing and empowering effect of both relationships.

Q.   *What is yoga exactly and why does it seem difficult?*
A.   The simplest meaning of the word yoga is union. When you unite with someone or something you will experience the uniting in your mind. When you keep thinking about someone or something it is as if you are mentally communing with them. There is a subtle communication with them which, when you meet, will turn into a form of words. We communicate and commune with others mostly through physical means, but we cannot do this with our spiritual parent, with God, as He does not take a physical form. Our communion, communication or union has to be subtle, through the vibrations that we emit as souls. This does not take many births to master, as some would have us believe, but it does take a little practice. This is because our consciousness tends to be filled with thoughts and feelings about other people, our families, our work, past memories, imagined fears, etc. We need to learn to drop these 'thought conversations' with others so that we can redirect our attention and vibrations. This also means learning how to make our mind and intellect quiet enough, and open enough, to receive, to hear and to feel His vibrations, His communication, and to be aware of His subtle presence. Meditation is the preparation, yoga or union is the

aim, a silent communication of vibrations is the process and a sense of communion is the personal evidence that the connection has been made. Ultimately it is an exchange of the energy of pure love.

Q.   *How can I know that I have made contact and it is not just my imagination?*
A.   If it is imagination the experience will not last long and its power will diminish quickly. You will not change in any way. A true and authentic communion with God is something that grows and matures with time. It gradually awakens the soul to what is true and a deep transformational experience of real love. This automatically gives the soul the power to overcome the negative traits and tendencies which have been cultivated over a lifetime.

A Personal Experience

It took me a little time to get used to the idea that God is an actual, individual Being, with His own personality, and that I could have a personal relationship with Him. I suppose meditation helped me to rebuild my self-esteem and self-confidence to the extent that I began to feel worthy of that relationship. And then, one day, I sat down and had a very deliberate conversation in my mind with God. I guess I just opened my heart and let all my feelings, fears and frustrations out in a flurry of thoughts. Anyway, after about fifteen minutes, I was feeling pretty good, unburdened, but not as if I had any mind-blowing revelations or encounter with the great One! So, I was just sitting quietly, beginning to think about going home and suddenly this wave of love hit me. It was almost unbearable but I knew instantly who it was. I was just totally lost, completely absorbed by light. It was so beautiful, and to this day it still moves me. That was the moment when I knew who the real love of my life was. That was the moment that changed my life. I didn't say anything to anyone – it was too personal – but I just felt like I had this glow coming from my heart, and I knew my eyes were transmitters because people looked at me just a little longer than they would normally have done.

Questions to - meditation@bkpublications.com

Journal Exercises

A. The Divine Letter

Imagine God has written to you. In what ways would your spiritual Parent's love for you be expressed? What would be His hopes for you? What would be Her expectations of you? Remember God sees only the best in you. Find a quiet spot, where you are undisturbed and write a letter that your spiritual Parent would send to you.

Once you have written and read what you think He would say to you...write your reply!

B. Making it Personal

Every soul has a personal relationship with the Supreme, we simply forget as we become distracted by physical life and relationships on our journey of many lives. In the process of restoring and personalising our eternal relationship with God he plays many roles, just as a good parent will play many roles while bringing up his or her child. Each role is an expression of different spiritual attributes and characteristics. Take a few moments to reflect on the primary roles that God plays in our life and identify the main attributes or characteristics which He expresses. For example in the role of Father He expresses the lawful side of his character as he shows the child respect and demonstrates how to live. In the role of Mother she expresses...

God in the role of:	Has the attributes and character traits of:
Father	
Mother	
Friend	
Teacher	
Companion	
Guide	
Lover	

Once you have completed the above contemplate each of these roles in your meditation/yoga. See Him playing these roles for you. Feel Her being in that role for you, then note what you feel exactly and how you are responding. Can you identify the spiritual attributes and character traits that it brings out from within you?

The Laws
and Philosophy
of Karma

Understanding the natural laws which govern the
mental and physical universe of action

There are three things that we all have in common:

awareness — of ourselves and others
relationship — the sharing and exchange of energy with others
creativity — the ability to produce thoughts, ideas, concepts and
feelings and express them.

The purpose of our life is nothing more than living life itself – to
be self-aware, to be creative, to express ourselves to our highest
potential and to exchange the energy of love with those around us.
But this cannot happen in the incorporeal, silent home of the soul.
These characteristics of life require action, a costume through which
to express ourselves and a stage on which to act. The physical
world provides the stage on which we can move, bring to life,
create, relate and express all that is within us. For each of us the
possibilities are infinite.

The moment we take birth in a physical form, we are constantly doing one of three things: acting, reacting, or interacting – sometimes all three together. There are certain laws which are intrinsic to action and interaction. They are not human laws requiring lawyers to interpret or police to enforce. They are natural laws which are constantly operating in every relationship. They are often called the Laws of Karma (action): acknowledged in Christian philosophy by the saying, "As you sow, so you shall reap", described by Isaac Newton as the Laws of Motion where 'for every action, there is an equal and opposite reaction'. The Laws of Karma remind us that whatever quality of energy we give out, we get back. This might not be exactly 'an eye for an eye', but if we give happiness to someone, it will come back to us; if we give pain or sorrow, it will come back, perhaps not today or tomorrow, but at some time in the future.

When we are reminded of these immutable laws of cause and effect, it awakens our awareness of our true responsibility. Most of us are conditioned by the idea that we are responsible for some of our actions, but not all of them. For example, we would consider ourselves responsible for the actions which bring our colleagues together for a task at work but would not consider ourselves responsible for the argument we have with a neighbour. We would consider ourselves responsible for driving our family safely to their holiday destination, but if we nearly have an accident because we were trying to get there quickly we might consider the other driver responsible for nearly causing the accident. If we sustain our family through our own enterprise and professional efforts we would take the credit, but if we turned to a life of crime to clothe and feed ourselves we might blame the inequalities of society or the formative years of a difficult childhood.

In our forgetfulness of this principle of karmic returns, we have learned to avoid taking responsibility for many of our actions. We fail to see the impact of our actions upon others and we fail to see that the real meaning of responsibility is our 'ability to respond'. Life can be seen as a series of responses which we each create in our interactions with other people and events. As is the quality of our ability to respond (energy given), so will be the quality of the returns (energy received). The Laws of Karma also serve to remind us that our circumstances and our personality today are the result of what we thought and did yesterday, last month, last year, perhaps in our last birth. Many people do not like this insight or find it difficult to accept because most of us have been taught that our destiny lies in someone else's hands or in the hands of fate or luck, about which we can do nothing. Karma is also sometimes referred to as the Law of Reciprocity. It is a law which teaches us that there is no such thing as luck and that whatever befalls us today is the result of our benevolent or negative actions in the past. If you spend a few moments reflecting on events in your life, without judgment or emotion, you will begin to see connections between actions and outcomes, causes and effects. When you see how all effects have their causes, you then have the evidence that this universal law is at work in your life at all times.

Two Dimensions of Karma

Karma has two dimensions: external and internal. We all radiate energy and whatever energy we send out in the form of our thoughts, words, attitudes and actions – as ripples into the larger pool of life – will eventually return in days, months or years. At the same time, if we think, speak and act in an angry way, we leave an impression or memory of anger within our own consciousness and the sanskara of anger is born (see Lesson Five). Within the sanskara is the recorded emotion and experience of our expression towards the object of our anger. If we encounter the object of our anger the next day, it will trigger the emergence of the recorded anger from within the sanskara. We then deepen the sanskara as we express more anger, even if we only 'think' anger. The emergence of this emotional energy from within our consciousness then stops us from interacting in a positive way. It clouds our mind and confuses our intellect, crippling and distorting our thoughts, decisions and behaviour. This often explains why we find it harder to connect and communicate with certain people in our life. Essentially we are carrying a negative image of the other person within our sanskara from a previous interaction with them. And when we see them again it invokes the energy within the sanskara, which then influences our ability to respond to them.

The record of our karma (actions) is entirely our own creation, carried within our sanskaras, like scars on the soul. These scars then express themselves as habitual behaviours. Just as any scars on our body require healing, so any negative sanskaras within our consciousness require healing. It is therefore important to be aware of the quality of our actions, which begins with the quality of our thoughts, which begins with the quality of our consciousness or state of being. Awareness of this cause/effect process, which begins within our consciousness, allows us to understand first: why we are experiencing discomfort today (due to low-quality action in the past); second, why we need to be careful not to reinforce any existing negative sanskaras with further negative thoughts/action; and third, how we may create positive karma or outcomes in the future.

There are essentially three levels or categories of action.

Negative action (vikarma) is motivated by consciousness of the body. When we identify with our body and think we are only our physical form, we think happiness is a physical experience and we seek self-gratification and fulfillment through sensual experience. Our senses are designed to consume external sources of stimulation, so we develop the habit of taking and forget that everything we take must be given back some day in some way. The resulting dependencies give rise to tension and anxiety, generating thoughts like, "Can I have more?" or "What if I don't get more?" Dependency is always a hair's breadth away from addiction. Any sensual addiction entraps the soul, inner freedom is lost and real happiness is impossible. There is always the possibility that whatever we become accustomed to being able to take or consume may finish, or cease to be available, and so fear is ever present. It is here that we find the birth of stress in its most common forms.

When our sense of self and our security are both based on our position, possessions, pay or another person, then life's daily events can easily represent a threat to any of these things, thereby affecting our sense of security in the world. The consequent fearful and angry thoughts and the actions which follow accumulate a negative karmic debt. Any actions motivated by greed or attachment are what we could call 'sinful' actions, where the meaning of sin is simply to forget who we are. When we forget who we are, our actions spring from an illusion of who we are, and those actions are therefore inaccurate and negative, often destructive. Our capacity to be loving, peaceful and contented is diminished. Although we grow accustomed to tension, dissatisfaction and being upset, we don't realise that these emotions have their roots in forgetfulness of the true self. Over time, the record of all thoughts and actions, which are driven by these states of being, accumulates within our consciousness and a heaviness sets in.

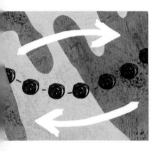

Negative action is also a result of misuse or abuse of one or another aspect in our life: of the body, of relationships, of wealth, of our thoughts, etc. Taken on a simple level, if we gorge ourselves on cream cakes and do no physical exercise, it is certain that we will gain weight at some point in our life. Our bodies are not designed to take in more calories than they use without producing a negative result. We are able to see the results of our actions on a physical level, but it is not so easy to see or admit the negative results of our actions on other levels.

Neutral action (akarma) involves routine tasks which do not normally adversely affect others: washing dishes, writing a shopping list, choosing what clothes to wear, etc. However, even these actions, if carried out in a state of body-consciousness, can easily become negative on a covert or subtle level and a further debt or heaviness may be accumulated.

Positive action (sukarma) arises from a state of being soul-conscious. We are aware that we are spirit and that we have spiritual energy at the core of our being. We are free from wanting anything from outside ourselves. We do not look for peace and happiness from outer conditions, as we now know and experience

them as inner states of being. We have reversed the flow of our energies from taking to giving. Aware that we are eternal and imperishable, we are not threatened by others in any way. We can see the best in everyone and encourage their full potential and their spiritual qualities to blossom. We are also able to move consciously into a spiritual state of being at will. We can be powerful, joyful, insightful or full of love by choice. We know that whatever spiritual state of being we choose, that state emanates towards others without effort. Our thoughts, attitudes and actions are all expressions of our state of being.

However, it's not that we become full of love or generous towards others because we want some positive energy in return. If we give with the subtle desire or expectation for a return, our motive and actions are not soul-conscious. In an enlightened state, while we 'know' that whatever we give will return to us, we are simply giving from our heart. It is the highest impulse of spirit. To be is to give. There are no conditions placed on our being.

The most significant actions carried out in a state of 'soul-consciousness' will always bring spiritual benefit to others. The greatest thing we can do for others is to help them to rediscover both their soul-consciousness and their link with the Creator. We do not attempt to force enlightenment on another or expect that they must accept this, but we can be instrumental in helping others to see how they can set themselves free from illusion and to reconnect them with the Source of spirit, with God. This is the highest karma.

Karma – The Universal Debt Collector

Whether we are a cleaner or a mechanic, a corporate executive or a king, we have all made the same mistake of losing our true self-awareness (soul-consciousness). This is why, at this present time when the world is in a state of transformation (see Lesson Nine), we all find ourselves with 'debts to settle' and some inner scars to heal, not only from this lifetime, but also accumulated from previous births. The web of karmic debt can weigh heavily within our consciousness. This explains why even those people who have an abundance of material wealth and physical comfort are often painfully unhappy. The burden of these karmic debts can also prevent us from finding true freedom, as the 'sins' of our past disturb our peace and our happiness in the present. If someone keeps coming into our mind, interrupting our concentration, or they trigger feelings of frustration or depression when we see or even think of them, we can understand that we are likely to have some outstanding debt with that person, and often there is a sanskara which we need to heal. Once again, there is an underlying lesson to be learnt or something that has to be changed. In these moments, although we may think we are free to think, say or do what we want, we do not have spiritual freedom. We are tied to our inner disturbance (sanskara) which has been triggered (not caused) by the outer event or presence of a person.

Freeing the Self

There are three methods of settling our karmic debts and setting ourselves free.

Staying Awake and Aware

The first is to increase the awareness of the self as soul and diminish the illusion that we are our body. This ensures that all actions come from an inner state of peace, generosity and benevolence, without any personal agenda or conscious desire for any return.[16] This requires the gentle effort of constantly reminding ourselves who and what we are – soul not body. Our identification with our body is so strong that it can be drawn like a curtain across our consciousness in a second. The path of the awakening spirit is therefore one of waking (awareness of self as soul) and sleeping (under the illusion that we are our body), waking and sleeping. We tend to fluctuate between the two (like dawn and dusk) until we find stability in soul-consciousness. This is why it is important to awaken and stay awake, and why it's important to give our mind and intellect good spiritual food and exercise every day to keep them fresh and alert. Being soul-conscious, and acting from that consciousness, naturally heals the scars (habits and tendencies) left by past actions based on illusion (body-consciousness). The evidence that our meditation is working is a lightness of spirit and an increasing easiness in our interactions with others. These are the signs that we are clearing our karmic debts. It is at this transitional stage that we will often find it helpful and supportive to be in the company of those who are also practising meditation, learning to be 'soul-conscious' and making the same effort to awaken and to stay awake. It gives us the opportunity to share experiences and learn from others. We will also be less likely to find benefit or make progress in the company of those who continue to focus mainly on the material world and who still see themselves only as physical beings.

Face to Face

The second way in which we can begin to settle our outstanding debts is by giving back to those souls from whom we have in the past 'taken' and with whom we now have some 'karmic account'. However, this can take time, especially if we imagine all the souls we have interacted with during many births. We are sure to have one or two people in our life right now who seem to have the capacity to press our buttons or just stimulate feelings of discomfort by simply being in our presence. If we are serious about 'waking up', we will not avoid these people, nor will we go looking for them. Instead, we can use these relationships as teachers and opportunities to learn about ourselves. We can ask ourselves, "What is it within me that is reacting to this person in this situation? Why am I creating this discomfort in their presence?" In this way, we will see and understand what we need to change within ourselves. We understand which sanskaras need to be healed and transformed. It will always come down to something connected with our own ego or attachment. Our inner healing will always begin with the 'letting go' of something. When we identify what that is and when we do 'let go', we find it takes the negativity out of our thoughts and actions, thereby breaking the negative patterns of exchange with others.

The moment we are aware that our own discomforts are self-imposed, we are halfway to self-change and the clearing of karma. The next step is to forgive ourselves, for wounding ourselves with our negative thoughts and actions, and to forget the past. When we do this work of inner healing, we automatically change our response to the person or situation previously triggering our discomfort. Our new spiritual response is like a new step sequence in our dance with

the other person and if we change our step they have to change theirs. Alternatively, they may be dancing the right steps and we learn to dance the right steps, too. Whatever the case, the saying, "When we change, the world changes", holds true. If they don't change, we will need to empower our own capacity to be patient and check that we are not wanting them to change in a certain way as a result of our own desires and expectations. If we do want them to change, it means we are trying to control them in a subtle way, which means we still retain a selfish motive. This always results in frustration and failure as it is not possible to control another human being.

Healing Power of God

The third and most effective way to heal and clear the burden of our karmic debt, both inside and outside, is through the process of meditation and yoga. In yoga (see Lesson Four), we establish a direct link with God, the Source of spiritual love, light and power. When we are directly connected to the Sun of spiritual energy, we can allow that energy to heal the negative sanskaras (habits and tendencies) within our own consciousness. As our energy changes, through our power of thought, we are able to send out that positive energy towards those with whom we have some difficulty (karmic account). In yoga, we open to the warmth of pure love and the light of eternal truth from the Source, healing our own spirit and liberating ourselves from the illusions which made us create wrong thoughts and perform wrong actions in the first place. The illusion was simply in seeing ourselves as limited, mortal, physical beings. This led us to believe that love, happiness and peace were physical and to be found externally, which in turn made us use others to get what we wanted. Healing has taken place when we experience ourselves as souls, unlimited, immortal, spiritual beings and children of the Supreme. Healing has become a reality when we rediscover our own internal resource of love, happiness and peace. Only then will we begin to see and perceive others in the same way. This spiritual vision transforms the quality of energy we give to others which then heals and transforms those relationships (see meditation in Lesson Six). Once we have fully healed our self-awareness, we can act as instruments to bring that light from the Source into the lives of others. By doing so, our intention to serve others spiritually has the effect of purifying our own motives in all areas of our life. The healing power of God is then available to others and to the world.

Meditation 10 – Healing and Settling

Our yoga or union with the Source is the most effective way of healing and settling our accounts of karma. The thoughts within the following meditation may help you to draw on the energy of the Source in order to heal the inner wounds and scars which are left by the negative karmas of the past.

I sit quietly in meditation...aware of myself as a soul...

In soul consciousness I reconnect with my inner peace...

I see the beauty of the many virtues of the spiritual being that I am...

There are natural feelings of love and appreciation for the self...

At peace with myself, I turn my thoughts to God, to the Sun of spirit...

I open my heart to the light of my spiritual Parent...

I feel the warmth of His presence and the light of His love for me
gently healing the wounds of the past that are buried deep in my
heart...

The wounds left by fear and sorrow, by sadness and anger dissolve...

Like iron being turned into gold, the Alchemist is doing His work,
and the deepest healing is taking place...

While I sit and absorb this healing energy from the Source I also
reflect that light out into the world...

The vibration of my reflection of His light and love touches everyone
I know and have ever known...

It is a light which also heals and transforms my vision of them...

I now recognise everyone around me as fellow souls, spiritual beings
on their own unique path, playing their own unique roles...

I also realise they too have lost their true self awareness...

With this new soul-conscious vision all negative memories and past
hurts associated with each relationship is willingly released...

The only important moment is now, and the past is forgotten...

The healing of forgiveness is complete, and the karma is cleared...

In this present moment there is a deep feeling of liberation...

In this moment there is a deep appreciation for the presence of God
in my life, and a humble acceptance of His invitation to assist...

The beauty of the Laws of Karma is understanding that if our
actions bring happiness and spiritual upliftment to others today, our
own tomorrows will be bright. It reminds us that our destiny is
firmly in our own hands and it starts with the creation of our own
thoughts.

Give Yourself Permission

Our personalities are essentially the combined habits of a lifetime, built on the combined habits of previous lifetimes which have left their mark as our inner tendencies, at the end of each birth. It may well be that habits such as becoming angry or upset, anxious and tense, have been with us for so long that they feel a natural part of our inner life, so natural that when someone says our true nature is not anger but peace, not fear but love, not aggression but acceptance, not anxiety but calm, it does not feel right. And even if it did feel right for a moment, we have become so attached to our old habitual moods, feelings and behaviours that we do not really want to change. It may even be the case that we have become so weak that we need help to change. It seems much easier to stay the way we are. As we begin to meditate and develop our spiritual practice, our view on this will fluctuate. When it does, imagine you are having a conversation with yourself and teaching yourself. Give yourself permission to be peaceful by nature, full of love[17] by nature, naturally content by nature, wherever you are and in whatever you do. After a while, you won't need to give yourself permission and you will find these states of being are there within you quite naturally at every moment. They are our original and eternal nature. Everything else is learned. In so many ways this course, like many other authentic approaches to spiritual awakening, is as much about unlearning as it is about learning.

The Creative Process

Karma shows us how all suffering is self-inflicted. At the spiritual level, suffering is caused by attachment. At the emotional level, it is called fear. At the behavioural level it looks like resistance. The process by which we create our own destiny is quite easy to see on paper, however it requires some checking to see if it matches the reality of our inner and outer lives. Here is the process in essence.

Sow an intention and reap a thought.

Sow a thought and reap a feeling.

Sow a feeling and reap an attitude.

Sow an attitude and reap an action.

Sow an action and reap a habit.

Sow a habit and reap a personality.

Sow your personality into all your relationships on your journey through life and you will reap a destiny.

Watch your thoughts!
Be aware of your intentions!

Our intentions stem from our beliefs about who we are, where we are and why we are here. If we believe we are physical and mortal beings, we will believe we are here to survive as long as possible. This leads to the intention to get what we think we need before others, which leads to competition, which leads to fear. If you know you are the immortal and imperishable energy of soul, then survival is no longer an issue and your intention expands to include, connect with and enlighten others. The service of others at a spiritual level becomes the highest intention in action. It is fully free from fear and can be seen as an act of love. This is why competition and spirituality are never found together.

Frequently Asked Questions

Q. *In the world today, we see many injustices and people suffering. How can we relate this to the Laws of Karma?*

A. In a world where everyone knows what everyone else is doing, as they are doing it, each day brings scenes and images of many apparent injustices. Whether it's in the office or on the television news, we see people suffering tremendous pain at the hands of others. Our sense of injustice is stimulated and it becomes easy to rise from our armchair in outrage against the perpetrators. In the process we ourselves suffer from our own self-created anger and perhaps hate. This process then becomes a habit and an inner pattern we begin to repeat, not only when we encounter scenes of global strife, but the moment someone at home or in the office does something similar. A button is pressed and we react with the same pattern.

What we forget, in both global and local contexts, is the history and geography of karma. Every scene and situation has a variety of related causes in both time (history) and space (geography). But we often fail to consider this. An understanding of the laws of action reminds us that whatever we give we get, and whatever we get is the result of what we have given. When we integrate this understanding into our awareness while we watch apparent injustices in the world, it defuses our outrage, lessening our pain. It's not that we sit passively and allow people to inflict suffering upon others, but it helps us to see that the greatest or highest contribution that we can make, to both the victim and the persecutor, is to help them remember who they are and help them rise above their anger and fear towards each other. Only in this way can we help them to liberate themselves from an exchange of energy that has perhaps been going on for centuries. But before we can effectively do this for others, it is

necessary to be able to do it for ourselves. Instead of taking the law
into our own hands (the desire for revenge), we can benefit everyone
around us by understanding and living according to the invisible
laws of cause and effect which define all human relationships.
Sometimes this is referred to as 'walking the talk', and it often
requires moments of reflection before action in order to discern the
consequences of any path of action. This capacity to stop, reflect
and consider, in a state of mental calm and with clear intellect, is an
essential attribute of all effective leaders. It is also what makes us
all potential leaders in life, every day.

Q.   *How do you know that your actions are creating negative
karma?*
A.   At the very heart of our consciousness, we have a conscience.
Our conscience is essentially our innate awareness of truth. From a
spiritual point of view, the truth of who we are as spiritual beings is
a core and eternal truth. If we consider ourselves to be anything
other than spirit then we will be thinking and acting against our
conscience, against our truth, which is like going against the grain of
spirit. We will feel something is not quite right. If one of the pistons

in our car engine is out of sync with the others, the engine will sound slightly strange. We immediately have it fixed, because we know that if it continues it may destroy the engine. If we do something that is out of sync with the truth, the voice of our conscience speaks to us. But we tend to ignore or suppress it, especially if we are having a pleasurable experience – we then create the sanskara or habit of ignoring our own conscience. The smoker hears that voice telling him to stop poisoning his body, wasting money and being addicted, but then ignores the voice or drowns it out. This only adds to the inner disharmony already present and both self-respect and self-esteem are slowly eroded.

Any action we do which springs from forgetfulness (body-consciousness) will trigger this inner, spiritual discomfort. Following the action, we might feel guilty for doing something we innately knew was wrong. Any form of guilt that is not induced by another person (that is, not a response to emotional blackmail) is the voice of our conscience calling to say that we are acting against the grain, something is out of sync. Our level of guilt acts like a barometer. It shows us when we are not aligned to truth. If we learn to pay attention, listen closely to this inner discomfort and the message it conveys, we will also hear why and how to make corrections.

Q.   *Why do we become moody?*

A.   At any one moment, we have the capability to feel something. Our feelings vary throughout the course of the day. Sometimes they are pleasurable and sometimes they are painful. What we forget to do is to choose our feelings consciously. Instead, many of us have become lazy and allowed our feelings to be dictated and shaped by people and circumstances. In other words, we have become influenced. Our swinging, changing moods are the result of the inner karma of becoming attached to things, people, ideas and circumstances. If we are attached to our job and we are made redundant, we will feel gloomy and our mood of doom will drain our energy just when we need to look for our next job with optimism and enthusiasm. Any form of loss will induce the mood of sadness which, if repeated over a long period of time, will turn into depression. When someone says or does something we do not like, our resistance to their actions and their presence leads to anger and ultimately rage. We feel these emotions first within our own consciousness.

When we think we are only physical entities and consider the world around us to be our source of happiness and joy, our moods will  fluctuate, even with the changing weather. But when we know who we are, and are stable in the awareness of being soul-conscious, our happiness and joy come from inside. We are stable in the face of praise or defamation, loss or gain. We are no longer moody and equanimity is our inner state of being. We are at the helm of our life, with our hand firmly on the rudder of our feelings. And while we cannot control the waves of the ocean of life around us, we can control and choose how we will respond to outer events and people. When we do, we will be able to choose what we feel, regardless of what may come to us. Life ceases to be a rollercoaster and becomes more of a cruise, less a hurricane and more a gentle breeze. We will truly be able to sing in the rain!

Q.   *Why don't we recognise our state of body-consciousness?*

A.   One outcome of the transition from soul-consciousness to body-consciousness is the distortion of the virtuous characteristics of the soul into negative traits. It all begins with the development of the ego. This occurs when the soul (self) becomes attached to and identifies with the wrong image of the self. The first and most powerful attachment is a misidentification with the body. Having lost our true self-awareness as an imperishable soul, we fall under the spell of the illusion that we are physical and therefore mortal. It is this illusion which gives rise to the thoughts and actions of taking, keeping, defending and protecting. It makes us think that survival is essential, that the major goal in life is the accumulation of possessions and a relationship based on mutual attachment. As a result of these beliefs, we see the birth and growth of five vices which then hold our spirit in their grip – ego, attachment, greed, anger and lust. Lust has many levels and is not confined solely to physical relationships. We lust after many physical stimulants – from music to movies, from meals to mates – little realising we are further binding ourselves and that we will have to settle the karmic debt, which is accrued as a result, at some future date.

Q.   *How can I be sure of what my intentions are?*

A.   We need to understand that every action, thought and feeling is motivated by an intention, and that intention is a cause that exists and must have an effect. If we participate in the cause, we must participate in the effect. In this most profound way, we are held responsible for our every action, thought and feeling, that is, for our every intention. It is, therefore, wise for us to become aware of our many intentions, to sort out which intentions produce which effects and to choose our intentions according to the effects that we desire to produce. But where does intention come from? Intention has its deepest roots in our sense of identity. If we think we are British, black or Muslim (body-consciousness), we will perceive the French, white or Christian as different and possibly a threat; so our intention will be to beat, avoid, overcome or defend ourselves against others. These are fear-driven intentions and must rebound some time, somewhere. See yourself as the eternal, imperishable soul, above and beyond such limited, physical identities, and you have nothing to fear and nothing to lose. This then allows the intention to love and respect others to become real in your actions and returned in time.

A Personal Experience

Understanding the Laws of Karma was a revelation to me. I'd spent my life in pain and most of my relationships were a walking disaster. They would start off OK, but then it was usually all downhill from there. Then I saw the ripple effect operating in my life and realised it's me, I'm doing this to me.
I'm getting back what I put out. Initially I was resentful – why didn't someone explain this to me sooner? And then it turned into a kind of relief and a 'so that's why' kind of feeling. Now I'm very careful about my thoughts and attitudes towards others. Now I make sure I don't accept others' pain. I accept them, but I don't consume their negative energy. And I endeavour not to take it personally when someone criticises or attacks me. Intellectually I know that their attack on me is really an attack on themselves, but in reality it's tough to be stable and compassionate, but I'm getting there. I'm still working on that one. Now I know what is a secret to most people – my inner and outer destiny is always in my own hands.

Journal Exercises

A. Life Action Review

Take a moment to write a short note to God as your friend, sharing with Him all the major negative actions which you can remember that you have done in your life. No need to go into detail. Just a short list. Then, when you are finished, fold it neatly, offer it to your Friend in a short meditation then...burn it. See the burning as a complete release from the past and all its karmas.

B. Mood Rerun

At the end of the week look back on the week and identify three definite moods that you experienced. Note the time, place and who was present. Then reflect on each one individually and look behind your mood to see the cause. Note down what you see.

C. Action Awareness

At the end of each day this week, review the day and recall five key actions in each day. Then categorise each action according to its quality in the grid below. In this way you increase your conscious awareness of the quality of your actions.

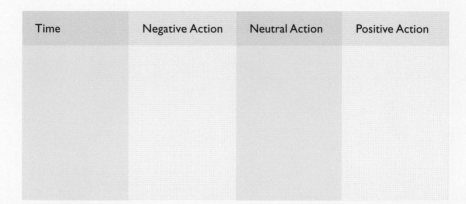

Time	Negative Action	Neutral Action	Positive Action

D. Future Karma

Karma tends to be a reference to the past but it also has an important futuristic dimension. What we do today will determine our life in the future. Take a moment to envision your future (in this lifetime) at a spiritual level, drawing on what you have learned in this course so far. Describe in detail your vision of yourself - what are you doing, what are talking about, what are you feeling, who are you with etc. Then stand back from your vision and ask yourself. What do I need to do today, at a spiritual level, to manifest my vision of my future?

The World Drama

lesson

8

Understanding the history and geography of time

While we may now be rediscovering and expressing our true spiritual identity through the practice of meditation and cultivating our personal relationship with God through the practice of yoga, how are we to make sense of what appears to be an increasingly chaotic world? How are we to find meaning in events that often seem bereft of meaning? A useful analogy would be to see ourselves as actors in an epic and complex drama. We, the souls, are actors and our bodies are our costumes. If we can extend this understanding into a larger context, we might see the truth in Shakespeare's famous phrase 'all the world's a stage'. Taking place on the stage of our world is an enormous, unlimited drama, in which each person has the opportunity to play many roles. Each day is filled with many scenes and each scene is an opportunity to create and play the most appropriate role to the best of our ability. Therefore, we are each hero actors with the opportunity to interpret the script of our own life. This is the deepest challenge to our creativity – the challenge of creating our own destiny. While it is our destiny to live the day, the year, the lifetime, we have free will as to 'how' we will live the day, the year and our lifetime. Each day offers us multiple choices as to how we can respond to the world around us and our ultimate destiny is governed by these choices. Our destiny is decided not by what happens to us or around us, but by how we respond to events and circumstances as we meet them.

We now know who we are (Lesson Two). We know the laws which govern our relationships (karma) with ourselves, others and God (Lesson Seven). We can now set about creating the life we choose. Many people do not like this idea of being the masters of their own destinies. Most of us have been taught that life is more about fate and luck, but these are simply ways of avoiding consideration of the potential of our life and taking the necessary steps to fulfil it. By resigning ourselves to a life of luck and fate, we conveniently avoid doing the inner work of becoming awake and aware of who we are as spiritual beings and the masters of our own destiny. This is why

self-awareness is the first step towards empowering ourselves, towards taking responsibility for our life.

Some of us are also taught that each of our lives takes a direction which is set according to God's will, so we should not be so arrogant as to think we can override God's plan for us by trying to do it our own way. This is a passive response which prevents each of us from using our free will to make any choice at any moment. While there is a master plan which is playing itself out on the stage of the world, a part of the plan is that we each have free will and the opportunity to know ourselves as we truly are. Built into our consciousness is the capacity to discriminate right from wrong, good from bad and to decide how we will act. These are divine attributes when they are used in the right way. They remind us that life is a creative opportunity to be all that we can be and an opportunity to help, encourage and empower others to be the same. If someone were to attempt to take away this right and the freedom to make our own choices, however small, we would probably fight to defend them. We only ignore our rights and freedoms when it is convenient, and it suddenly becomes

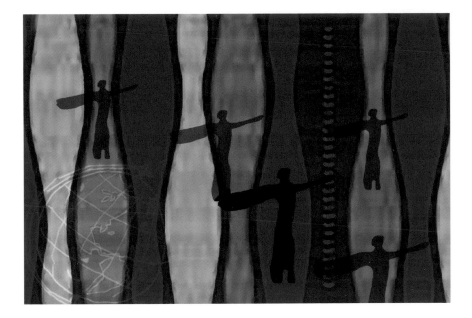

convenient when we do not want to face up to our responsibilities for ourselves, or the consequences of our own actions within in our own life. The right to choose and the freedom to decide are the deepest responsibilities both towards ourselves and towards others because, as we saw in the last lesson, every choice and every decision has consequences.

In a world where we learn more about how to incapacitate ourselves, by seeing ourselves as victims, the beginning of true self-empowerment is when we fully realise that we can write our own script. It is also a moment when we are reminded that we have no right to write anyone else's script. This insight alone can set us free from one of our most entrenched habits, that of attempting to control others. This habit is always a wasteful use of our time and energy, which can now be deployed to focus fully on our own life and our responsibility to create and play our roles in whatever way we choose, and to our highest potential.

The metaphor of life as an unlimited drama, a stage on which we all come to act and interact, create and co-create, and the true perspective it provides, also helps us to understand more accurately the complete history and geography of time. To the eternal soul, time is a paradox – it exists, and yet it does not. As we play our various roles on the stage of life, we are 'in time' and yet we are eternal beings, 'beyond time' and its constraints. It is only when the soul enters the corporeal dimension of time and space, movement and change, that creative expression is possible. At its deepest level, our movement from a dimension beyond time into the co-creation of a drama within time and space reminds us of the supreme paradox: we do have free will and yet our destiny is already set. This paradox cannot be understood by logical, linear thinking, but as an intuitive insight into the true nature of time or the true nature of the journey of the soul into the material world and out again. This is a cyclical movement and not a linear one. This paradoxical insight is further clarified when we explore and understand the laws of time which govern our corporeal world.

The Laws of Time

There are two basic laws governing the passage of time in this world. Firstly, time moves in cycles, as do the events that give rise to our awareness of the passage of time. Secondly, everything new becomes old. These two laws help us to understand the 'complete human story' or the history of time (change), and they shed light on why the world is in its present state.

We use time to attempt to measure change (that is, our experience of the space between events). Our measurement of time begins with the changing position of the planets around the sun and a day becomes the basic unit of measurement. One year is measured by the cyclical

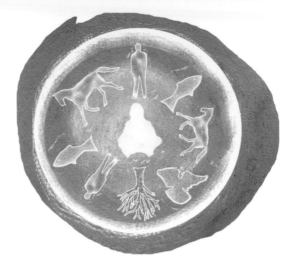

movement of the planet around its own axis while orbiting the sun. Here lies the key to understanding that the movement of time in our physical world is always cyclical. The cycle of the day, from dawn to daylight to dusk to night, is a movement that repeats with absolute constancy. A larger cycle is that of the seasons – from spring to summer to autumn to winter – which also revolve in the same way. When we stand back from the 'big picture' of human history, we see an even larger cycle. But to focus fully and see that picture, we first need to understand and integrate the second law of time.

In each of these cycles, we also observe that everything new becomes old. Nothing ever starts old and becomes new. From cars to carpets, philosophies to religious movements – all move from a state of newness to a state of decay. When we translate this principle and process to the world as a whole, we can more easily understand why we live in an 'old world': overused, misused, tired and where many areas are simply worn out. This process is sometimes known as entropy. The Law of Entropy describes the movement from order to chaos, where energy in a closed system runs down when it is not replenished from a source outside that system. In the context of our physical planet, the sun sustains and re-energises the systems of nature every day, and so the Earth is sustained. Only in the past century has our exploitation of the natural world started to outpace its capacity for renewal. We now use the trapped energy in our

physical world much faster than the sun can replace it through the Earth's biological systems.

When the Law of Entropy is translated into our values and attitudes, we can perhaps begin to see why, as individuals, we feel worn out, tired and old 'in spirit', even while we may still be relatively young in physical age. We can also begin to understand why material values hold greater sway than spiritual values, why negative attitudes easily prevail over positive. In fact, the entropy of our values has followed the same pattern as the entropy of our world environment. The outer manifestation of our decaying values can be seen in the decay of our cultures, where our values have become almost totally superficial and transient. They are frequently based on the material and not the spiritual or moral dimensions which used to prevail in almost all cultures. It is the decay in our values which has largely contributed to our exploitation, pollution and general disrespect for the natural world. Stepping back a few hundred years, we can easily see that the so-called 'civilisation' of any culture or society has, in most cases, marked the beginning of its moral decline.

When we discern and accept this movement from new to old and combine it with the acceptance that we have not been spiritually renewing ourselves, it reveals a very different understanding of the events we have been taught to call history. As we look back down the ages, we find there have been revolutionary moments in human thinking which seem to have transformed life on Earth for the better. Deep philosophical insights, groundbreaking scientific discoveries, thousands of practical inventions and the development of global communication have all contributed to the rise of the illusion of progress. While we may be able to communicate across vast distances instantly at any time or produce mountains of information, smoother cars and smaller telephones, human relationships are in crisis and the wisdom to make better choices is one of the scarcest

commodities. While we may be enjoying tremendous technological progress, it seems clear that we are not enjoying the development of healthier, more loving and harmonious relationships with ourselves, each other or the planet – and yet this is in accordance with the law of new to old. The ancients knew and understood these laws. This allowed them to predict the future – not in specific detail, but in general terms. It allows us to understand more accurately where we are now in the context of the cyclic history of the human race.

The Four Ages of Change

In the mythology and legends of almost every ancient race, including the Egyptians, Greeks, Hindus, Mayans, Incas and Aborigines, there are extensive references to a period, some four or five thousand years ago, when Earth was Paradise. Remembered as the Golden Age, Garden of Eden, Atlantis, the Dream-time, these legends all point to

a time when the world was beautiful and new – heaven on Earth.
In his book, Memories and Visions of Paradise, Richard Heinberg
describes how he came to see and understand the significance of the
Paradise Myth. Seeking to understand the true nature of our
collective journey to this point in time, he discovered a common
theme in world folklore of a vanished Paradise and the quest for its
restoration. He recalled the Myth as follows:

*"Nearly all ancient peoples and traditions of a primordial era have a
common memory of a time when humanity lived a simple yet magical
existence in attunement with nature. The ancients said that this
Golden Age came to an end because of some tragic mistake that forced
the separation between heaven and Earth. They said the rupture
between the two worlds precipitated a descent into separateness, fear
and greed that characterise human nature as we know it today. They
said that it was only after the change in the human mode of being – the
Fall – that the Earth was subjected to horrendous global catastrophes
whose geological, climatic, and psychological impact erased nearly
every trace of the former 'golden' condition."*

In both Greek and Indian mythology, the cyclical movement of human life on Earth is depicted by four distinct phases or ages.

Golden Age (dawn/spring) – remembered as Paradise, heaven on earth, over 4,000 years ago when humanity was one kingdom and there was complete purity of spirit and harmony in all human affairs. Suffering in any form or at any level is unknown.

Silver Age (day/summer) – still relatively like Paradise, still unity, but the purity of soul and matter are beginning to wane. Suffering is still unknown.

Copper Age (dusk/autumn) – the loss of spiritual awareness and the descent into consciousness of the body (see Lesson One), the beginning of separation and fragmentation of humanity, the birth of suffering and conflict. The ego begins to reign in the minds and hearts of men and women. Love is distorted by the ego into fear.

Iron Age (night/winter) – the dark night of the soul and the darkest period of the world, a time of greed and avarice, conflict and war at all levels of human activity.

Where are we now?

In the context of the complete human story, we are now at the darkest period in human affairs. Our spiritual power is at its lowest ebb. We are no longer one world but fragmented into over 180 nation states. We fight over resources, pollute our planet and have lost respect for almost all levels of life, most of all, our own. All this is simply because we have forgotten who we are and why we are here. Like children playing all day in the woods until night has descended, we realise that we don't know where we are or how to get home. We start to argue and fight with each other and small groups break away and go in their own directions. Many of us feel an overwhelming sense of being lost. Our cries for help take many forms, from drugs to crime, dishonesty to deceit, from outright violence to the inner breakdown of mind and body.

The entropy of spiritual values and, as a consequence, human relationships worldwide is now plain to see. There is now a global culture with the predominant characteristics of fear instead of love, vice instead of virtue, sorrow instead of happiness, conflict instead of harmony. These are all symptoms of ill health at the spiritual and mental levels. When they get a foothold within us as individuals, they result in physical disease and, when they become the currency of our relationships, we kill each other (mentally and physically). However, it takes more than sunlight to renew and revive the energy of human affairs. The only way we can heal, renew and replenish our spirit is to turn to face the Sun of spirit and, in that spiritual relationship, be open to receiving the pure light and love which reawakens, heals and renews the soul. The healing of our relationships can only happen when we, as individuals, realise that we are sources of love and are ready to simply be ourselves, untainted by any negative experiences of the past.

The Fifth Age

Although some parts of the world have never been more physically comfortable and materially prosperous, we are now at the darkest point in the cycle of all humanity. Winter winds of greed, conflict and exploitation now blow through all aspects of life on Earth. It is at this time that our spiritual Parent hears and responds to our collective cries for respite and relief from the pain and the fear that we ourselves have created. Like a good Parent, He intervenes at this, the only time during our entire journey, to tell us the whole story – who we are, what has happened to us and how to find our way home. He reveals the complete picture and, as a consequence, sets us free from our illusions and collectively created delusions.

One of these deceptions can be found in our understanding of freedom. While we think we live in a free world – free to fly, buy, say almost anything, anywhere, any time – it is not real freedom. It is only physical freedom. The source of our personal pain, and the darkness that permeates our relationships, is within our own spirit.

The pain is there because we make ourselves slaves to people, circumstances, objects and ideas – even our own expectations. We build our own prisons and the bars are defined by our attachments, false beliefs and misconceptions. If we are to live in a better, more harmonious world, something which most would want, we have an opportunity to play our part in that process. That means letting go of our limited supports and our dependencies on the transient things in life, like our possessions, position and prestige. That is not to say we give everything up and find a cave in the hills! It means changing our relationship with these things, awakening to who we really are as imperishable souls on a grand adventure, and allowing ourselves to be guided back to our spiritual home and our spiritual Parent. It means allowing the healing of our own spirit to take place.

The Past is the Future and the Future is the Past

A circle is not a circle unless the line turns perfectly consistently to join up with itself. A cycle of time is not a true cycle unless it repeats itself identically. The repetitive cyclical movement of time,

that we call human history, means the past is also the future and the future is the past. From such a perspective, we can become aware of a fifth age, the age we are now in – the Confluence Age – a time of transformation and transmutation from old to new, from night to day, from Iron to Gold, from vice to virtue, from fear to love. From the end of one cycle to the beginning of another. This insight into the significance of this time period now releases us from wondering why the world seems to be so full of pain and suffering, as we can now understand that karma is being cleared at both the individual and collective levels, debts are being paid and atonement has begun. Knowing this, we find it easier to detach from

the numerous negative scenes brought to us by the media, while staying focused on settling our own karmic debts. At the same time we are available to those around us when they need a little help to settle their own karma in the easiest way possible.

When we recognise the precise and exact nature of cyclic time, we can also joyfully expect and work for a new dawn. For this to happen, great changes must take place in the context of human affairs. It is a process of change that can only begin from within the individual. Just as we have been responsible for the degradation of the physical environment of our world, so it is we who must initiate the repairs. When we understand that all causation is downward (from spirit to mind and then to body or matter) we realise that it is our own spiritual awakening and purification which can transform our world at all levels – first our identity, then our state of being, then our intentions, then our attitudes and then our actions. As we turn to face the Source of love and light, the degenerating process of entropy is halted and reversed. The soul returns to its original pure and loving state. The consequence is a transformation of the inner world of consciousness which, in turn, is reflected in the transformation of the outer world that we all share. When we change, the world changes.

When we see and realise the significance of this current age, the fifth age or the Confluence Age, we also find greater clarity in our life's purpose. It becomes obvious that the world will not become a better place through more resistance or conflict; this only adds to the sum of fear and anger in the world. To fight for peace is one of the most

blinding contradictions which grip the human mind. To think that
peace comes from conflict, or that conflict is necessary to achieve
peace, is to think right comes from wrong. Deep transformation is
an incognito process within individual souls. Through meditation,
we awaken and restore our true, peaceful selves. Through the
practice of yoga (union), we absorb the light of truth and love from
the Source and we are spiritually empowered. This we can then
share with others. As we radiate our spiritual energy and reflect the
light of the Source into the world in gentle and unassuming ways,
the effects of our self-transformation reach out to others as an
invitation to do the same.

The nagging questions which must enter most minds at least once in
a lifetime (such as "Why me?", "Why here?" and "Why now?") are
answered – our highest purpose is nothing more than to be
ourselves, true to ourselves and available to serve others and our
natural environment. The greatest service is to help others know
themselves as they truly are and to assist in reconnecting them to
the Source. All energies in the world ultimately dance to the tune of
spirit. This is why simply sitting in meditation, generating and
radiating vibrations which are peaceful and loving, can help to heal
others and the world itself.

Meditation 11 – Spinning the Wheel of Eternity

We are not separate from time. Time is life and we are time, because we are life. In meditation, it is possible to get a deep sense of our journey through time, and perhaps many lives, not as individual images or specific scenes, but as an intuitive sense of a long distant past which, by virtue of its being invoked into the 'here and now', will also be the future. We are each a participant in the cycle of life, while at the same time, as immortal and eternal beings, the cycle of all time is within us. Here are some thoughts to meditate and reflect on, which may assist you to create an awareness of times past and your own unique journey into the future.

I visualise a wheel...
I am at the centre of the wheel...
It is the wheel of all time...
I am completely calm and totally still as I watch the wheel of time rotate around me...
Like a revolving screen, it shows me many scenes, evoking the feelings of many deep memories within me...
It's as if I can feel what I was like when I first came onto the stage of this world...
I was a pure and loving being...
My innocence of spirit meant my nature was playful and pure...
I danced and laughed naturally with everyone...
I created beauty in all that I did and in all my relationships...
And then, very slowly, imperceptibly at first, the dance of life began to lose the spring in its step...
As the wheel of time continued to rotate, I became more conscious of the physical world around me...
More aware of the shape of my physical body...
With the passing of time I was drawn and attracted to my own physical body and then to the physical forms of others...

As my soul consciousness ebbed away it was replaced by consciousness of the body...

As my sense of mortality grew I began to build barriers and create fear, and the first moments of suffering arrived...

The dance of life began to lose its harmony and rhythm...

The lightness of my spirit faded and my heart slowly became heavy as I filled my tired mind with lazy and troubled thoughts...

Then I began to search outside myself for some relief...

I prayed, I cried out to God, I searched, and I could find no solace in external and limited comforts...

The conflict within me began to finds its way out into the world...

A darkness pervaded my consciousness as many forms of sorrow and suffering became residents of my mind and heart...

I begin to live through the 'dark night of the soul'...

My energy levels are depleted, for the first time my mind knows despair and my body becomes ill...

Then, just as the lowest point is reached there is a sudden glimmer of hope...

The Light of truth responds to my soundless cries and comes to awaken and enlighten me...

I see myself now, bathing in the light of the love of the One...

The lost energy of my long and tiring journey is being replenished...

I feel the deepest spiritual comfort as the Comforter of all hearts nurtures and empowers me back to my original state...

I am reunited with God, my eternal Friend and dearest Companion...

My heart soars once again as I gradually remember who I am, and rediscover the truth of why I am here...

Laughter and love return to my thoughts and feelings...

I can now see my own return to this point from where it all began...

And I can sense the wheel beginning to turn...once again.

Frequently Asked Questions

Q. *What is the simplest way to understand time?*

A. Essentially we create time in our attempt to measure our experience of the space between perceived events. Time passes only because we perceive and experience change. Change is only a series of events. So time is our experience of the speed of events. This explains why time seems to be moving faster today, because both the speed and the quantity of events are increasing. And it seems even faster if we participate in those events. Modern media allow us to observe hundreds of events from all over the world, every day. To observe is to participate. If you want to slow time down, learn to detach and be the observer of events. If you want to stop time, meditate and be in your original, timeless consciousness. Today, however, it is as if we fear time when we hear ourselves say, "Quick, time is running out!" or "Hopefully, there will be more time tomorrow!" or "Hurry up, we need to save time!" Ultimately time is our life: it cannot be saved or lost, but must be lived now. This is where free will begins – we can choose exactly how we spend our time at any moment.

Q. *Why do we find it so hard to recognise and transform ourselves, to awaken to who we really are?*

A. One reason is we all have the tendency to spend most of our time in the past, reliving our memories and succumbing to nostalgia. Look back on your average day and you may find around 80% of your attention went into the past. Not only do we try to relive the past, but we also attempt to change it! We attempt the impossible and, in so doing, we live in very small cycles where tomorrow tends to turn out similar to yesterday, and then we wonder why we do not have the power to change our lives. It feels like we do not have free will. The past cannot be relived; it cannot be changed. The past is like a filing cabinet. When you arrive at work every day, do you step into the filing cabinet and spend the day there? The past is a great resource for learning and an occasional resource for useful information, but it is not a place to live. We can build on the old, but we cannot rewrite it. The future is the result of what we think, feel and do today. If today is the same as yesterday then tomorrow will look and feel like yesterday and in this way we feel we are stuck in a rut. We need to let go of the past if we want the future to show up! The past is past. Drop it and keep dropping it. This inner exercise will eventually allow you to be present now. And life only happens now!

A Personal Experience

At first I found it hard to understand the concept of eternity and then a spiritual colleague said, "Why don't you experiment and imagine that everything you do and say today is eternal?" The most amazing day unfolded where everything intensified and became more significant. I had such an awareness of the role I was playing and I was careful to play each scene in the day's drama to the best of my ability. It was a joy to be alive. It gave me an understanding of what living was really about. I forgot about the past as I focused totally on the present moment. Doing this made me realise that I had been playing an old record over and over again. That day gave me the chance to try something new and to appreciate where I was at that moment. I can never thank my colleague enough for opening my eyes. Not only did I find transformation in that one day, but I have tried to continue the experience as often as I can each day. This has helped me to progress. I use my experiences of the past to build my present with the awareness of the consequences in the future. I no longer feel depressed and even look forward to waking up each day.

Journal Exercises

A. Spinning the Cycle

Go back over the meditation practice for this lesson. This time, without reading or trying to remember the written ideas, simply sit quietly and create the sequence for yourself - new to old to new - fall and rise and fall and rise. Play with the cycle in your intellect, as if you are spinning the history of time. What do you 'see'? What do you feel? What does it show you? Note down your experience. As you make your notes, stop occasionally to reflect and allow yourself to see deeply.

B. Life Cycles

Cycles can be found at all levels of life. Even in your own life you will find cyclical patterns. On a separate piece of paper draw a cycle, divide it into four quarters with a cross - note down the characteristics of each stage as you contemplate the cyclical process of each of the following:

1. Phases of your own life
2. A Relationship
3. An Organisation
4. A Community

The Tree of Life

Spiritual understanding of how the dance of
life on Earth has evolved

O ur perception can either cloud or clarify our understanding.
At this point in time, within the story that is human history, we
need a perception which provides us with both clarity and accuracy.
One effective way to perceive and understand the drama of human
life in its completeness is through the metaphor of a tree. A tree
symbolises the process of growth and expansion – from a tiny seed to
a huge, solid, structure of trunk, branches, twigs and leaves – and
then decay and renewal. The seed of the tree of all life is the
Supreme Soul, or God. He is the only one who knows the whole
story from His vantage point in the incorporeal dimension. He has a
complete and continuous awareness of all time and space. Just as
the whole blueprint of a tree is contained within the seed, so the
whole knowledge of how the drama of life on Earth unfolds is
contained and known by Him.

The initial stage of growth is the sapling, or the Golden-aged phase, when the drama begins to unfold. It is a time when spirit and matter are pure. As in nature, when new growth is full of vital energy, the soul is also in its most powerful state of consciousness. Souls are arriving to take on a physical form in a pure, new world. There is complete balance and harmony within each individual and between all people. It is the age of gold. It is heaven on Earth. It is Paradise within the consciousness of the soul, which is reflected within the world itself. Both human nature and the natural world have a perfect beauty.

As the sapling expands and strengthens, the firm trunk symbolises the Silver-aged phase. While the number of souls taking birth increases gradually, there is still a feeling of oneness and unity of all (unlike the separateness that will manifest with increasing overpopulation in more recent times). It is still heaven on Earth and yet its inhabitants do not say, "This is heaven!" as they have no lesser experience to compare it with. It just is. The purity, innocence and unfettered happiness is a radiance emanating from every soul. However, as the soul plays its part within the expansion of the drama of life, the sparkle of this pure innocence wanes imperceptibly through action and interaction, and through the accumulation and weight of experience. This accumulation of karma

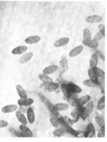

gradually weighs so heavily within all souls collectively that, once again, there is that most significant moment in all of human history – the descent into negativity brought about by a startling shift in consciousness.

Often documented in biblical terms as the 'fall' or referred to in literature as 'Paradise lost', this is the time when innocence is lost. It signifies the moment when there is a loss of natural spiritual expression and exchange, and a transition into body-consciousness. The self/soul begins to identify with the form that it

occupies and animates. Spiritual amnesia sets in and the soul
succumbs to the illusion that it is the body. This is the end of the
Silver-aged phase and the beginning of the Copper-aged phase, when
we lose our true consciousness of the self and the mastery of our
physical senses. We begin to indulge in physical sensation. We lose
the joyful impulse behind all that we create. We begin to believe we
are mortal and to think like mere mortals. We become conscious of
death as a real probability, as something terminal rather than
transitory. Mortality becomes a fearful reality and love is distorted
into fear, clouding our capacity to see and think in harmonious ways.
Confusion is known for the first time. Dilemmas develop between
right and wrong, good and bad. The dualities, which were once only
a feature of our external environment, become a reality within our

consciousness. Sensual experience becomes the source of happiness and, as a consequence, external 'things' take on a greater value than inner spirit, giving birth to attachment and greed, the impulses which lie behind all division and separation. Our unity is shattered. Suffering and sorrow enter human experience, where before there was only harmony and love.

At this point, some souls begin to wander and search in different directions to find answers and solutions to this new, strange malaise. The quest for truth begins, as does the search for a special Being dimly remembered as the Supreme One or God. While some races mistakenly invest both the sun and nature with divinity and look towards both for salvation, it is during this period that special messenger souls incarnate to play their part in this, our corporeal drama.

At different times and places, the 'prophet souls' – Abraham, Buddha, Christ, Shankaracharya and Mohammed – take birth. Each brings a specific message of a spiritual quality, an aspect of truth, needed at that point. Their role is to demonstrate this quality through the example of their own lives. Their intention, as 'leaders by example', is to help restore harmony to humankind. While their actions are their message they also remind those around them of the eternal truths, where truth is defined as that which never changes. As the story of humanity unfolds, almost every soul will follow, at some stage on their journey, the legacy and teachings of one of the messenger souls. Abraham provides us with moral and spiritual laws; Buddha's focus is on non-violence and detachment; Christ emphasises the importance and power of love and forgiveness; Shankaracharya demonstrates the power of spiritual and physical purity; while Mohammed reminds others to remember only One. Some listen, some follow, but it is only at the end of their

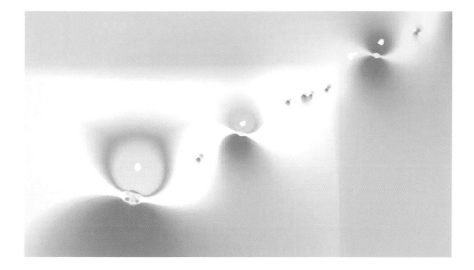

auspicious roles that what they said and did is recorded in what will become religious scriptures. These scriptures, and the philosophies which they contain, become the basis of the different branches of the tree of life. Each branch becomes a religious path, with its own set of beliefs and interpretations of universal truths.

Gradually, as time passes, as more souls take birth and the population increases, the numbers of followers on each branch increase. The original message of the 'prophet souls' and the belief systems which are created through the interpretations of their followers are institutionalised. Organisational structures and systems begin to grow, taking on a greater importance than the original truths which they enshrine. The purity of the original message is diluted and polluted. Like everything else, the growth and expansion of each branch of each religious philosophy is taken through its own Golden/Silver/Copper-aged stages. As one of these laws of time (see Lesson Eight) demands that everything new becomes old, each religion begins to fragment and separate into sub-branches as individuals interpret the original truths 'their way', leading others in differing directions. This growth continues into the

Iron-aged phase, the night of each religion. This is the time when each religious philosophy and its foundation begin to fragment into what will be hundreds of schisms, sects and cults.[18] In our metaphor of the tree of life these schisms/sects/cults can be likened to twigs, rather weak and delicate compared with the branch and trunk, and sensitive and susceptible to the slightest breeze of different ideas and beliefs. Hence the divisiveness and the conflict we see within modern sectarian religion today.

When the soul lost its true self-awareness and fell under the spell of body-consciousness, the energy of spirit became polluted. The natural love and peace of the soul was distorted into fear and anger. Virtue became vice. In contrast to the truth of love and peace as expressed by the prophet souls, we now see a thousand forms of irreligiousness. Unspiritual behaviour and the vices of ego, anger, greed, attachment and lust pollute every soul to some extent. As a consequence they are now rampant in all areas of life on Earth, including our institutions.

So here we are now in the Iron-aged phase of our world drama. A steady stream of new souls has continued to enter the corporeal world. The world population has increased gradually over several thousand years, eventually exploding exponentially during the last hundred years. The consequence of an increasing world population, combined with the entropy of human virtues and values, means there are now tremendous social and economic tensions, alongside an increase in mental and physical disease. The natural resources of the world strain to sustain over six billion people.

And yet, it's just fine. It's exactly how the drama of life is meant to unfold. It is already written in the script!

Evolution or Creation?

When we perceive and understand the growth and development of humanity in this way, that is, from new to old, from light to dark, it throws a new light over the concepts of evolution (a relatively new theory initiated by Darwin) and creation. When we recognise, either rationally or intuitively, that we do not come up from the Stone Age, but down from Paradise, we begin to awaken to the truth of our journey. We do not evolve to a higher consciousness. In fact the opposite is true. In our fall from grace, we gradually lose the purity of our consciousness, our spiritual awareness dims and it becomes an effort to discern what is right from wrong. When we understand the cyclical nature of this process, we also see that 'creationism' is also not totally accurate. Instead, we see the process of recreation and renewal, as the Source of spirit, the Seed of the human tree, steps in to initiate the process of purification and transformation, which marks the end of one cycle and the beginning of a new cycle. Everything in life proceeds in cycles.

Progress or Regress?

As a metaphor for the way that human life on Earth has developed to inhabit the planet, the tree allows us to hold the 'big picture' in our awareness. Using this big picture as a reference, we can see and understand why things have happened the way they have, and why the world is the way it is today: from one world to over 180 nation states; from pure and loving beings to fearful and aggressive beings; from an harmonious relationship with matter, in which we respect and care for the physical environment, to a relationship where we are slaves to material experience and try to control the physical energies of the world; from a world where we used to have all the time in the world for each other, to a world where we prefer to spend time with our technological toys; from a world where our hierarchies reflected their true meaning as a 'sacred order', held in place by love and respect for each other, and, most especially, for our elders, to a world where all forms of hierarchy are challenged and anarchy often reigns; from innocence to corruption; from joy to depression; from day to

night; from love to fear; from heaven to hell. Contemplate the tree as a dynamic symbol of life on Earth and you may find it awakens deep insights into the human story – at the same time explaining why things are the way they are today and will be again tomorrow.

When we begin to realise the significance of this time now, some of our deepest beliefs, prejudices and judgments begin to disappear. As we see the deterioration of human behaviour over time, we can see our regression and we might not hold so fast to our belief that we are progressing. It is much easier to believe in progress than admit that the quality of life and living is slowly decaying. This inability to recognise the entropy of energy at all levels of energy (physical, mental and spiritual) in the world is a sign of a kind of collective denial, another symptom of our sleepiness at the level of awareness.

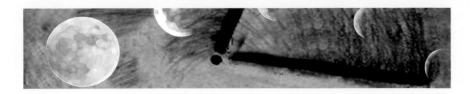

Under closer examination we might also see how our belief in competition as the sustainer of human progress is actually responsible for much of the fear and conflict in our modern world. In a more awakened state we might realise that the only way to restore unity and live together in peace is to choose not to compete with anyone for anything but to offer the hand of co-operation.

When we see the nature of the expansion of humanity, as symbolised by the growth of a tree, we not only understand why the movement from new to old, from strength to weakness, prevails around us, but we can also see how recreation and renewal takes place. An old tree is fully grown, destined to die, but not before its seeds release potential new life. And, in the tree of life, this is the role of God, the eternal Seed. The new tree is a spiritual one; its creation and emergence are not out of nothing but out of the re-creation, renewal and replenishment of the present spiritual energy within the old tree. We are that energy. As we turn to face the Sun of spirit, receive the light of love and truth, we are renewed and replenished. Through our connection with the Seed, the Supreme Soul, we become ready to create and serve the new growth.

Living within us there is a deep memory of our arrival for our first birth, the first chapter of our corporeal adventure. While this memory lies in the past, when we understand the true nature of time as a cyclical movement in time and space, it also lies in the future. In this sense, to remember this deep past, this original experience, is to invoke our future. To remember the time when we were pure, loving and totally content is to bring that state of consciousness back to life and into our conscious awareness now. When we restore and sustain the purity of this consciousness, we influence not only our own attitudes and behaviour but also our relationships with each other and the world around us right now. In this way each of us has the capacity to influence the world in a positive way, simply by altering our state of consciousness.

The methods to 'allow' this to happen are meditation and yoga. Meditation is the method to access the deepest levels of our own spirit where we find our original peace and purity. Yoga is the method to open the heart of our self/soul and allow the Sun of spirit to enter, awaken and heal. It means that we stand on the brink of a new world, a new beginning, if we so choose – if you so choose. We can choose to stand and live in the Iron Age, to deny our own light and live in these dark times according to dark ways, or we can choose to stand and live in the Confluence Age, the age of transition, the age when the light of truth re-enters the world. When we do, we may see that what looks like utter chaos in the world today is simply part of the inevitable process of renewal. The old house must be torn down, with all the dust and dirt involved, before the new house can be built. And as the old house is being flattened, the architects are quietly working out of sight, designing and perfecting the plan for the new dwelling.

We have the choice to stand and shout and complain at all the dust and noise, resist the developers and the decay in the faint hope that the cracks can be filled and what is broken can be patched up. Or we can stand with the architects of renewal, co-creators of a completely new world. Spiritual architecture is deep, invisible, incognito work, and only God, the Chief Architect, knows precisely how the new dwelling will emerge. Why? Because He has seen it all before and He remembers very clearly! If, in your meditation, you can be quiet enough, still enough, you can do the same.

Meditation 12 – In the Beginning

Life is an eternal interplay of three energies – soul, God and matter. Soul and matter are not created as they are eternal, but they do lose their purity over time. Gods role is to purify and renew. The Creator, in the truest sense, is the 're-creator', the purifier. The role of the soul is to assist. This is made easier when we understand the whole of creation and see our place within it. We each have a deep subconscious memory of our arrival in this physical world. It is a special time for the soul as the world is a new and novel experience. Like the experience of an innocent child each moment is filled with delight and discovery. The following meditation may help you to invoke a memory of that time when every feeling was pure and powerful, and when you the soul were the master of your mental abilities and physical senses.

With your body relaxed, remind your self that you are a soul, a being of pure, spiritual light... With your soul-consciousness restored you are now at peace within yourself...
On the vehicle of one pure and powerful thought, you return to the incorporeal home of silence and peace... You are aware of being in the presence of the Supreme Soul, the One who is the Seed of the tree of life, the One who not only knows you, but who knows the whole story... For a brief moment you too are able to hold the complete history and geography of the human world drama in your awareness...
It is an unlimited story created by the players themselves... You see yourself with Him at that moment, just before the first moments in time – the first moments of a new performance of 'the drama' of life on earth...
In that moment you feel the overwhelming urge to go

towards the physical, corporeal world...

It is as if you know that it is there that you will fully express your self and know yourself...

You intuitively sense that life awaits you in another world...

And in one thought, in one second, you are there...

You are in a new physical form...

The world around you is bright and beautiful, a rainbow of vibrant colours...

A pure delight cascades though your whole being...

What you see and hear and feel is a wonder to behold...

Your form is also radiant and beautiful...it is your perfect form...

Your whole being is awash with a rainbow of vibrant energies - the energies of greatest happiness in life...

You feel an incredible lightness... a serene contentment...a pure joy to be alive...

You see around you your companions for the journey...

Though you have not met before you recognise everyone you meet...

The meeting of eyes is also the meeting of hearts...

The echoes of this world are made only of laughter...

Every movement, every interaction with another, is filled with the magic of pure play...

We are woven together in a tapestry of life that is perfect and beautiful...

This is paradise...

In every face of every encounter you see the radiant beauty of spirit...

There is only light and warmth and love and joy... and it is everywhere at all times...

Each one plays their own special note...

Hearts and minds dance in an effortless harmony with each other...

Together we create the symphony of life...

Together we dance the dance of our eternal tale.

Words on paper are the least effective way to describe the possible experience that you may have with this meditation. It is less about words and images and more about feelings. Deep within our consciousness we all retain the first pure and perfect feelings of our first birth. This meditation is less about thinking accurate thoughts of who and what we are, and more about being so quiet, so still inside, that we are receptive to the deep memory of those original moments. As you allow those moments to emerge and experience those original feelings, they have the effect of transforming both your understanding and experience of what it means to alive now.

Frequently Asked Questions

Q. *Can you tell me more about the transition from the Silver Age to the Copper Age to the Iron Age?*

A. The end of Paradise (the fall) is the beginning of the Copper Age. It would have been marked by the beginning of philosophical enquiry and the search for the truth of how life and the world functions. This enquiry is motivated by the loss of inner and outer harmony. Imagine yourself in ancient Greece, sitting around the fire under the stars late at night with friends and family. The young ones are listening to the old ones as they pass on the wisdom of the ages through myth and legend. It is this wisdom of right understanding, right thinking and right living that maintains the balance and harmony of society. Not far away, there is another group discussing why the world is the way it is, why people do what they do. This group is trying to work out why there is an increase in sorrow and suffering. They are the philosophers in a process of inquiry. They are trying to understand how the universe works. One day, a few philosophers become tired of all the talk and intellectual inquiry and they decide to 'do something'. They begin to study the material world in all its forms and variety of phenomena. They start to fathom the rhythms of nature and the movement of the planets in an attempt to find mechanisms, meaning and purpose. Scientific inquiry is born and wisdom gives way to the gathering of knowledge.

Over one hundred elements, the development of electricity and, several hundred years later, the appliance of science spawns technology. Knowledge gives way to information. In the matter of a few short decades, everything that can be quantified and measured is reduced to sets of digits and fed into a machine for lightning transmission in massive quantities across vast distances. Information gives way to data. Take a moment to reflect and ask yourself at which level do you currently share with others, converse with others? Is it at the level of wisdom, knowledge, information or data? For most of us it is at the level of information. Information is mostly gossip with little or no value. What we all need more than ever is truth and wisdom, the two commodities in shortest supply today. You can now clearly see the absolute dilution of our values as we now evaluate the worth of many modern organisations according to their data resources. The more data rich they are the greater the value they have! From wisdom, to knowledge, to information, to data – this is progress, isn't it!?

Q.   *What is the Confluence Age exactly?*

A.   The Confluence Age is more a state of consciousness. It is an awareness of how all worlds – spiritual, mental and physical – are renewed and recreated through the transformation of the self/soul to the soul's original pure qualities of peace, love and truth. To make a personal commitment to this renewal and purification of the self, and to bring the light of truth into the world, is to stand in the Confluence Age. To decide to continue sustaining the mistaken identity that the self is a physical body, and all the behaviours and suffering which that brings, is to remain in the Iron Age. The simplest way to see it as an interplay of energies. When the soul loses its purity of consciousness and falls under the illusion that it is a material body, the vibrations of the soul change. They become slower and heavier. The energy of matter follows. The energy of molecules and atoms change their frequencies and become heavier and more solid. In time this increasing heaviness of spirit is what sustains the increasing heaviness of matter. Enter the Source of spiritual energy to rejuvenate the soul and restore its purity of being. This can occasionally feel a little chaotic internally. Matter follows with a process that appears to be equally chaotic, but is simply a reordering and a returning to original forms. The Confluence Age is the meeting of these three energies - soul, God and matter - in a process of transformation and renewal.

A Personal Experience

OK, I wasn't on the streets throwing rocks at the government; I wasn't an activist, but I was a hater, a resister. And then one night I got it! The big picture suddenly crystallised. I suddenly saw that it's all happening exactly as it should, and that resistance is not only futile, it is very unenlightened, spiritually naive. Apart from the fact that you empower whatever you resist, you are trying to interfere with the outplaying of a natural process, not to mention trying to write other people's scripts. I could see the environmental protesters making two vital mistakes, two wrong assumptions. They assume the planet could come to an end and that they themselves will lose their home, which really means their efforts are essentially selfish. And they assume they themselves are mortal. These two wrong assumptions generate the fear which motivates their actions of resistance. But the truth is that we never end and the planet never ends. This was a big realisation for me – we are eternal and the planet is eternal. We might try to wipe each other out, but Earth abides and it has unlimited power to heal itself. The sun is the source of that power. Suddenly I was able to drop the fear, end the inner struggle, even though it was largely mental, and begin to live in love, live from love. And just as suddenly I saw that that's the only energy that can bring positive change. regardless of all the 'apparent' injustices we are shown and see each day.

Questions to - meditation@bkpublications.com

Journal Exercises

A. Seeing the Big Picture

Meditate on the symbol of the tree and contemplate its meaning. See
if you can read the drama of life. Visualise the growth of the tree of
life from a seed to sapling to a mature tree. See the tree of life go
through its seasons until it is fully grown and at the end of its life.
See the process of final decay and the new tree emerging.   Can you
see your place in it? Can you see your role and purpose during this
particular phase of intense, significant change and transformation?
Note down your most interesting insights and realisations.

B. Inside Out

Take a blank sheet of paper and draw a tree of life (or find a picture
of one) and then label the various parts of the tree (roots, trunk,
branches, etc.) with what you think are the specific spiritual qualities
which emerge from within the soul at different stages/phases of its
journey through the time and space of the drama of life on earth.

What Next? A Spiritual Lifestyle

The source of this Raja Yoga Meditation Course and how to support your meditation and spiritual development with the correct lifestyle

Congratulations on the completion of the Raja Yoga Meditation Course. As you have probably noticed, there is a little more to meditation than just learning a specific technique. At its deepest level, the understanding and practice of Raja Yoga is a pathway to personal enlightenment and true freedom of spirit. Fully understanding and realising the significance of the insights and the wisdom within this course will obviously take more than a few weeks. But even if the deeper spiritual aspects have not yet found complete acceptance in your mind and heart, at the very least, you have found a basic practice of meditation that can help you be more peaceful, positive and powerful in your practical life.

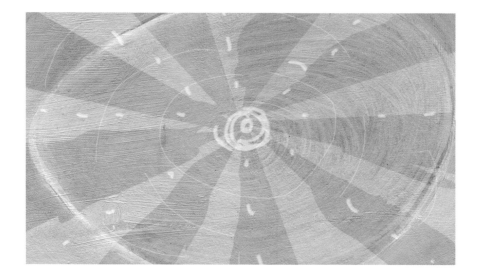

For those of you who are interested in taking your study of Raja Yoga further, it may be useful to know a little more about how the Spiritual University was started and the source of the knowledge and understanding contained in this book. Furthermore, if you feel that it may be an appropriate path for you to continue to explore, there are also some lifestyle recommendations which can ease your way towards that end.

The Brahma Kumaris World Spiritual University teaches Raja Yoga in over five thousand centres in more than eighty countries. The University was founded in 1937 by Brahma Baba. Born in 1876 into a humble home, the son of a village schoolmaster, Brahma Baba was brought up within the Hindu[19] tradition. However, he did not follow in his father's footsteps and instead entered the jewellery business, earning a considerable fortune as a diamond trader. As a businessman, he maintained a highly respected position within the local community and was known for his philanthropy.

At the age of sixty, when most of his colleagues were planning their retirement, Brahma Baba entered the most active and fascinating phase of his life. Over a period of several months in 1936, he felt the need to invest more time in quiet reflection and solitude. Then one day, while in a meditative state, he felt a warm flow of energy surrounding him, filling him with light and revealing to him a series of powerful visions. These visions continued periodically over several months, giving new insights into the innate qualities of the human soul, revealing the mysterious entity of God and explaining the process of world transformation. The intensity of the messages conveyed was such that Brahma Baba felt compelled to wind up his business and devote himself to understanding the significance and application of this revealed knowledge. The sound of the words ringing in his mind seemed new, yet felt so true and real. He was aware that he was receiving both the visions and the insights directly from the Source.

This Raja Yoga Meditation Course is based on the revelations that Brahma Baba received. In essence, they include the following aspects of wisdom:

- The real identity of the self as soul. The soul is the conscious spiritual entity that animates the body. The soul is eternal and indestructible.
- The identity of God, the Supreme Soul, and His location in a dimension of light beyond the physical world, and His form as a point of light.
- The key faculties of the soul – the mind, intellect and sanskaras.
- Control over these faculties is lost when we lose awareness of our spiritual identity and nature. This is the reason for all suffering.
- The immutable Laws of Karma define our destiny according to our thoughts and actions.
- Life on Earth can be likened to an unlimited drama – an eternal interplay between soul, matter and God where, for the most part, God does not interfere.

- The complete history of the human race is a story of this interplay within time and space. This interplay is cyclic and not linear. The cycle continues to turn.

- This time period now is the Confluence Age – the period of transition from one cycle to the next, when God intervenes and purifies the soul, thus reversing the process of entropy at a spiritual level.

- The evolution of life on Earth is like a tree that slowly grows from the Seed, the Divine Source (God), and becomes as large and diverse as we see today. Entropy accompanies the expansion of the human drama, which accounts for the period of vice and widespread violence that we witness in the world today.

- All the main religious movements are the attempts to institutionalise the message of the founding souls. These institutions, like everything else, also become degraded in time.

The final thirty years of Brahma Baba's life were dedicated to the establishment of a spiritual university and to the teaching and empowerment of others. At no time did he ever consider himself to be a guru. In fact he discouraged such titles, staying very much in the background and working quietly at the world headquarters of the University in Mt Abu, India. He always saw that his main role was to serve as an instrument for the Supreme, allowing the Source of spirit to use him to communicate the unique knowledge which is both the heart of Raja Yoga and the foundation of the University's work worldwide.

The living skills that he taught have stood the test of time. He entrusted leadership of the organisation early in the University's establishment to young women. They are now in their seventies and eighties, and have become beacons of love, peace and happiness in a world increasingly troubled by disordered relationships, greed, addiction, anger and violence.

Brahma Baba died in 1969 at the age of ninety-three. At the headquarters of the University in India, the Tower of Peace stands as a tribute to the invincible spirit of an ordinary human being, whose greatness was to accept the role of instrument to bring the universal spiritual truths of Raja Yoga to the wider world and to establish a spiritual university which could serve the world.

One of his greatest legacies was the simplicity of his lifestyle. As you will have gathered, the insights, knowledge and practices of Raja Yoga are all integral to a process of spiritual awakening, transformation and empowerment. Regular daily meditation is the foundation of sustaining our spiritual development. However, even the foundation needs to be supported and strengthened by a lifestyle that is conducive to our spiritual growth.

In order to reap the richest and the sweetest fruits from your meditation and yoga, here are some recommended lifestyle practices which are proven to help. None of them are compulsory, but they have all been tried and tested during the last sixty years by experienced meditators and yogis in both the East and the West.

Early Morning Meditation... Every Morning!

Early morning, before the day begins in earnest, is the best time for meditation. We are fresh and find it easier to focus and concentrate our thoughts. It helps us 'calibrate' our energies, making sure we set off with the right intentions and motivation for the day ahead. Try to give yourself exclusive time, before going to work, in your meditation space at home, rather than on the train or in the car. A half-hour session before breakfast is ideal to start with.

One of the reasons why many people find meditation difficult at first is they try to meditate on their own. It is not impossible, simply a little harder when you are in the early stages of learning. It helps a great deal to meditate in a group. The atmosphere is collectively created, there are fewer distractions and the company of others is supportive. Raja Yoga meditation is practised by regular meditators every morning at around 6am in all Brahma Kumaris Raja Yoga centres worldwide. If you would like to try a morning session, contact the nearest BK centre on the address list at the end and ask for the centre nearest you. Or see the international address list at www.bkwsu.com for a complete list of main centres worldwide.

There are also many other courses and workshops held at each centre which you can use to support your ongoing development, including this course. If you have enjoyed this course book and feel your spiritual development would benefit from meditation practice, attending this course at a Brahma Kumaris centre is recommended.

Diet and Nutrition

In caring for our body, our diet requires deep consideration. A vegetarian diet is recommended for both moral reasons (karma) and health reasons. While many people fear they will not get enough protein from a vegetarian diet, there are millions of vegetarians who have survived and thrived on a meatless diet for many decades.

With an understanding of the power and effect of vibrations (thoughts), attention is also given to the quality of our consciousness as the food is prepared, ensuring only the highest spiritual vibrations enter the food during preparation. Addictive and harmful substances like alcohol, non-prescription drugs and tobacco are avoided, as well as other ingredients that have a powerful effect on the body and, consequently, on the mind (for example, garlic and onions).

Meditation is used to empower the self to release any unhealthy eating habits and achieve freedom from any addiction.

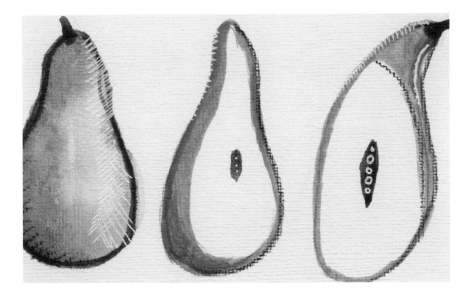

Rest and Relaxation

Providing rest and relaxation for the body is as important as it is for the mind. The timing and extent of physical relaxation is obviously dependent on personal metabolism, as well as professional and family responsibilities. Regular exercise is also vital to well-being. A practised meditator can also lessen his or her dependence on sleep.

Spiritual Study

Taking time each morning to meditate, study and understand spiritual principles and values, provides both mental and spiritual nourishment for the day to come. Following the morning meditation at each BK centre, there is a period of study, including a short talk, to provide the mind and intellect with good food for the day ahead. Following completion of this Foundation Course in Raja Yoga Meditation, centres welcome people from all walks of life and at all levels of spiritual development to join the morning sessions.

Good Company

Aware of the influence of other people, the spiritual journey is best made in the company of those who are positive and encouraging by nature – ideally those who are also on a similar journey. If we feel we are being unduly influenced by those who prefer to express a negative outlook on life, perhaps we need to review the time we spend with them. This can present us with a challenge if that negative person is in our family or at our workplace. In such a case, it is useful to perceive that person not as a problem or obstacle to our spiritual progress, but to see each encounter as an opportunity to practise what we are learning – our enemies, adversaries and negatively inclined companions then become our teachers. The principle here is: take care, because the company that you keep can easily colour your thoughts, feelings and eventually your personality.

Loving Relationships

As the practice of meditation takes you to a deeper understanding of truth, it is almost inevitable that the meaning of love will be explored at some stage. Love is our primary need, as well as the greatest gift that each of us can give. Love is the highest currency of human relationships. In many ways, the aim of the spiritual quest is simply a return to an awareness and expression of true love. When the human capacity to love is fully realised, three levels of loving are possible – physical, mental and spiritual. In current times, two of these levels are largely unexplored territory in the vast majority of relationships. The one that receives almost all our attention is the physical. In our modern culture, sex has become synonymous with love and this perception leads to unbalanced, unhealthy relationships. As we can now observe on a daily basis, it results in almost total fixation on our bodies, the growth of negative behaviour and attitudes towards the body, selfishness and the disappearance of spirituality. This is one of the deepest reasons for the increase in levels of fear, abuse and violence in society today.

If there is a recognition of this deteriorating state of affairs in our relationships and it is placed alongside our new understanding of our true self as spirit not body, we can see why many people on the path of spiritual development choose to devote a period of time to celibacy. This allows us the time and inner space to remove and heal habitual and sometimes addictive attention on the physical. It gives us the opportunity to learn to know and love ourselves spiritually. This then becomes the basis of 'true love' for others. A period of celibacy, which is freely chosen and fully understood, makes it much easier to raise the level of our consciousness from the anchors of the corporeal to the true awareness of self as soul. Much healing and renewal takes place during this process, as we rediscover true love at the mental and spiritual levels.

Achieving a Balance

A balanced, spiritual and fulfilling life is like a table. It stands on four legs and if one leg is shorter than the others then both balance and equilibrium will be difficult. The four legs or pillars of a spiritual life are:

1.   *Daily meditation and yoga*
Daily meditation and yoga provide the means to explore, discover and reconnect with oneself and with God.

2.   *Daily spiritual study (knowledge)*
Daily spiritual study provides the right quality of nourishment for mind and intellect, the two key faculties of the soul.

3.   *The inculcation and development of virtue (dharna)*
Giving some time each day to the conscious development of our character (virtue) helps to eliminate any negative traits (vices) and enhances our ability to build positive relationships.

4.   *The service of others (seva)*
A life purpose based on some kind of service is the foundation of personal growth through the practice of giving. Finding an appropriate way to use our now growing spiritual power and understanding for the benefit of others is the most satisfying way to use our energy today, while ensuring prosperity for all tomorrow.

Enhancing the Quality of Your Spiritual Attributes

If, as a beginner of meditation, you have been practising the meditation exercises throughout this book, you are beginning to become proficient at creating and experiencing feelings of relaxation and inner peace. Even as an experienced meditator, it is likely you will have found a deeper understanding of yourself in the simplicity of the spiritual truths which underpin this approach. The territory of spirit and spiritual understanding is both infinite and unlimited. It is not the territory of spiritualism, but simply the rediscovery of the deepest values and virtues of the human soul. The innate attributes of the soul (peace, love, truth and happiness) give the soul its power. The power of the soul cannot be quantified, only experienced and revealed through the 'quality' of these attributes and the forms they are given by the soul itself. For both the beginner and the experienced meditator practice, patience and a gentle persistence guarantee the rediscovery and expression of one's spiritual attributes and the ability to give them inner and outer form. When we choose

to be peaceful, we reconnect with our inner peace and create the spiritual form of peace within our self. However, what is the quality of that form, what is the quality of our peace? Is it a superficial quality that is easily broken with unexpected changes in our external circumstances, or is it a deep peace which is stable even in the face of fierce criticism from others? Only we know the quality of our spiritual forms.

In this final meditation, we will focus on the spiritual attribute of happiness and its relationship with peace and love. Before you begin the meditation take a moment to contemplate the truth about happiness. You now understand that real happiness is not an external stimulation; it is not the result of acquiring something, or of receiving good news. True happiness is not relief from suffering, nor is it the achievement of a goal. All these are externally dependent, where happiness is confused with stimulation, excitement, achievement, acquisition or relief. You also know that happiness is not a future promise. It can only be experienced now. Perhaps a better way to describe spiritual happiness is **contentment.** This comes from a complete awareness and acceptance of the self as we are now at an internal level, and an acceptance of 'what is' at an external level. The highest happiness is **bliss** which can be experienced only when the soul/self is totally free of all attachment and dependency. With this spiritual understanding of 'happiness' in the background, let's begin our final meditation.

Meditation 13 - The Form of Happiness

Sit comfortably and relax

Remind yourself of your spiritual form as a soul - a point of light...

Now stabilise yourself in your inner form of peace...

Fully release all your concerns, anxieties and worries, and allow all of your self to become deeply peaceful...

Be aware of yourself creating a peaceful form...

Feel the vibrations of your peaceful form radiating outwards into the world...

First into your body...then into the room...then into the community ...and then into the wider world...

Be aware that the vibration of your peaceful form is a gift...

Consciously give this gift of peace with the intention of calming and relieving the peacelessness of others...

As you radiate the power of your peace into the world you do so with great love...

As you give the gift of peace, with love, you are aware that you are able to serve others, help others, in this subtle but vital way...

This awareness invokes a new sense of meaning in your life and a deeper form a happiness within your heart...

It is a happiness which takes the form of contentment...

This contentment of the heart flows through your whole being...

You realise that your happiness does not live alone...

The true form of your happiness always has with it two of it closest companions ...the true form of peace and the true intention of love.

Our innate spiritual attributes of peace, love and happiness, combined with our awareness of truth, can be likened to the primary colours of the soul. While the soul can take these inner forms, it is only when they are mixed together that they emerge though our attitudes and behaviours as virtue. Virtuous action restores balance and harmony to our inner life and to our external relationships.

Frequently Asked Questions

Q. *I am a very busy person. How can I follow all these spiritual practices in today's fast-moving world?*

A.   As with everything in life, if we really want to do something, we will make time for it. If we have become addicted to the actions of a negatively-oriented lifestyle, it might take some time to change our everyday habits. However, it is not too difficult to take one aspect at a time. Practise it, observe the effect on the quality of your life and your relationships and adapt it to your own needs. Once you become stronger, and your sense of spirituality deepens, you will find that adopting these practices becomes quite natural and doesn't really take much effort. You will begin to appreciate all the gains you are accumulating as you recover your soul-consciousness, enhance the quality of your thinking and by doing things in ways that are more creative and enriching.

Q. *Isn't the idea of serving others for people who have a vocation in life?*

A.   From a spiritual point of view, at its simplest level, service means changing the quality of your thoughts, feelings and attitudes. This helps you improve the atmosphere around you which in turn enhances your relationships with others. Service in this context is not a question of imposing or pushing, but rather of leading by example and showing others a more positive way of living. In this way, simply by being in the company of others, you are serving them spiritually.

Q. *Why do I need to meditate daily?*

A.   Practice makes perfect! Just as when you learn to swim, ride a bicycle or drive, etc., by having regular lessons, so with meditation: the more you practise, the easier it becomes.

A Personal Experience

I remember when I took the meditation course I was in the company of someone who was actively seeing me as a soul. I saw such kindness in her eyes, an expression that I hadn't seen for such a long time. It was like I had re-awoken to unconditional love. When I left my first class, I felt fresh and with a renewed sense of hope. I knew then that I had stumbled across a new way of living that was going to change my life for the better – and for good! It was sometime later that I realised this 'seeing' of each other as souls had the potential to transform a relationship and probably the world. It was even later that I realised the deepest purpose of my life. It wasn't to do anything, it was simply to be myself. It sounds easy but it's the hardest thing in the world. It dawned on me that this meant complete non-violence at all levels of thought, word and deed. Up to that point I'd been following the spiritual disciplines out of a combination of faith, fear and obedience. But then I realised exactly why they were necessary. It was as if I needed to follow them before I could understand how they were supporting my return to being me. Now I fully choose them and see them not as disciplines but as integral and natural parts of my life.

Questions to - meditation@bkpublications.com

Journal Exercises

A. Virtues and Values

Take one of the following virtues or values per day and spend five minutes contemplating its meaning and its application during the day. Which of the 'primary colours' of the soul are hidden within that value/virtue?

Harmony
Forgiveness
Trust
Flexibility
Courage
Gentleness
Freedom
Understanding
Benevolence
Patience
Enthusiasm
Tolerance
Serenity
Caring
Co-operation
Generosity
Integrity
Humility
Respect

Then at the end of the day, create a 15 minute meditation for yourself along similar lines to the Form of Happiness meditation.

B. New Days

Organise your day. Use the table below. Firstly, in the left-hand column brainstorm all the changes you would like to make and new activities you want to build into your day in order to incorporate your meditation practice and spiritual study. On the right-hand side create a rough timetable for the day that now includes those ingredients in a prioritised list.

Changes and New Activities	Priority Timetable

End Notes

1 *(Page 20)* While the words 'spirit', 'self' and 'soul' may be open to interpretation, particularly when translated into other languages, in this book, self, soul and spirit are used with essentially the same meaning - an energy that is distinct from the tangible, physical energies of the body and the material world. In the learning of meditation it is not considered to be necessary to embark on a philosophical discussion of these words at this stage of the study.

2 *(Page 21)* Even where education has progressed to the point where pupils and students are encouraged to 'think for themselves', there is still a widespread lack of attention on teaching people how to take responsibility for their thoughts and to move away from the culture of blame.

3 *(Page 41)* Non-living here has the meaning of not being able to function on its own with any indication of intelligence or ability to think, etc. Not to be confused with inanimate.

4 *(Page 41)* Living here means that there is the ability to think or awareness or consciousness of its own capabilities.

5 *(Page 42)* There is a simple expression that encapsulates the essence of who we are, Om shanti. In the context of this course Om shanti is used and interpreted as follows: Om means 'I am' and shanti means 'peace'. Together, they mean, "I am a soul and my true nature is peace." We can use this expression to remind ourselves of our true identity at any moment. Please note that this is not a mantra that you need to repeat endlessly without effect. It is often used when greeting like-minded people, to show that your interaction is based on a spiritual level rather than on the shortcomings of having consciousness of the body. We can also start and finish our meditations with this expression, which helps to put us in the correct frame of mind.

6 *(Page 50)* During this course we may use the words self, spirit, consciousness or soul to describe the same thing – that is, what we essentially are. These words refer to the living, conscious energy that we are, as opposed to the non-living energy of our bodies that we animate.

7 *(Page 60)* We use this word in the same vein as the word 'brethren' was originally used: to mean both male and female. The energy of the self/soul is without gender. However, the qualities or attributes of the soul can be considered to be a balance of masculine and feminine.

8 *(Page 63)* Negative thoughts usually arise as projections onto others and it is easier to blame than to take responsibility for our own actions. It means we have not yet learned to be fully responsible for our own thoughts, feelings and actions and prefer to blame others.

9 *(Page 77)* Further explanation of this term is given later on in the lesson.

10 *(Page 78)* Not to be confused with the brain, which is a physical organ.

11 *(Page 79)* Used here in the sense of being in control of the self; not being influenced by external factors.

12 *(Page 85)* We will come back to this idea in a later lesson.

13 *(Page 104)* Understood here to mean our limited attempt to measure our experience of the space between two events.

14 *(Page 107)* Obviously, the awareness being described here is far from the self-centred awareness of someone whose whole approach to life is narcissistic. Here, we are focusing on the pure, natural and original energy of the soul.

15 *(Page 134)* The word 'brotherhood' is used here in the same way 'brethren' was used in the past, to mean family or community, something unrelated to the issues of male/female.

16 *(Page 151)* Admittedly, only God can be described as truly altruistic; even a mother expects the return of love from her children. Here, however, we are assuming the difference between conscious and unconscious motives.

17 *(Page 156)* Many people interpret the use of the word self and self-love as narcissistic and leading to selfishness. From a spiritual point of view nothing could be further from the truth. If we are not able to accept, appreciate and love ourselves it will be impossible to accept, appreciate and love others. We have learned to hate, fear and to create anger towards others. These are not natural states of being. Learning at a spiritual level is as much about unlearning the habits of negative thought and action which we may have adopted from watching others as it is about learning something new. Meditation and yoga are seen as the most effective ways to learn how to love again, which begins with the self.

18 *(Page 192)* While the terms 'sect' and 'cult' are often lumped together, there is a difference. A sect is used to refer to an offshoot of an existing religion, usually with a religious leader at its head, whereas a cult is a gathering of people who usually follow the beliefs and instructions of a charismatic leader. It is often the case that cults are led by strong, dominating personalities who frequently negatively influence their followers. Sects, on the other hand, are more often than not a group of deeply spiritual/religious people who are following a 'diluted' or 'variant' message to the one brought by the original religion they have moved away from.

19 *(Page 206)* Raja Yoga is not a branch of Hinduism.

Recommended Reading

Following this introduction to Raja Yoga Meditation, which is taught worldwide by the Brahma Kumaris World Spiritual University, the following books are recommended to enhance your meditation practice and deepen your spiritual understanding.

The Atma Point	Anthony Strano
Practical Meditation	BK Jayanti
Companion of God	Dadi Janki
Pathways to Higher Consciousness	Ken O'Donnell
Discover Inner Peace	Mike George
Memories and Visions of Paradise - Exploring the Myth of the Golden Age	Richard Heinberg
God's Healing Power	BK Jayanti
Soul Power	Nikki de Carteret
Learn to Relax	Mike George
The Soul Illuminated	Judith Shepherd- Pemmel
Mission of Love	Roger Cole
Healing Heart and Soul	Roger Cole
The 7 AHA!s of Highly Enlightened Souls	Mike George
InsideOut	Dadi Janki

All the above books (with the exception of Memories and Visions of Paradise) and a variety of Meditation Commentaries and Meditation Music which support this introduction to Raja Yoga Meditation are available from

Europe: **www.bkpublications.com**
Americas: **www.bkwsu.com**
Australasia: **www.brahmakumaris.com.au**

International Addresses

If you would like to visit a Brahma Kumaris Centre and attend a Raja Yoga Meditation course please check with nearest centre below and find the nearest centre to you.

**INTERNATIONAL
CO-ORDINATING OFFICE**

Global Co-operation House,
65-69 Pound Lane
London NW10 2HH
Tel: 020 8727 3350
Fax: 020 8727 3351
✉ london@bkwsu.com
Website: www.bkwsu.com

78 Alt Street, Ashfield,
Sydney NSW 2131, **Australia**
Tel: (+61) - 2- 9716 7066
Fax (+ 61)- 2- 9716 7795
✉ indra@brahmakumaris.com.au

Rua Dona Germaine Burchard,
589 Sao Paulo/SP 05002-062,
Brazil
Tel: (+55)-11-3864 3694/2639
Fax: (+55)-11-3872 7838
✉ brazil@bkumaris.com.br

897 College Street, Toronto
Ontario M6H 1A1, **Canada**
Tel: (+1)- 416 - 537 3034
Fax: (+1)- 416 - 537 1319
✉ toronto@bkwsu.com

17 Dragon Road, Causeway Bay
Hong Kong SAR, **China**
Tel: (+852) - 2806 3008
Fax: (+852) - 2887 0104
✉ rajainfo@rajayoga.com.hk

74 rue Orfila, 75020 Paris,
France
Tel: (+33) -1- 4358 4427
Fax: (+33) -1- 4358 3813
✉ bkfrance@wanadoo.fr

Pandav Bhavan,
25 New Rohtak Road
New Delhi 110005
Karol Bagh, **India**
Tel: (+91)-11-2362 8516/2367
Fax: (+91)-11-2368 0496
✉ bkpurity@vsnl.com

Toa Mansion Apt. 612, 1-30-15
Numabukuro, Nakano-ku
Tokyo 165 - 0025, **Japan**
Tel: (+81) - 3 - 5380 4169
Fax: (+81) - 3 - 5380 4179
✉ tokyoinfo@brahmakumaris.or.jp

Global Museum for a Better
World, Maua Close,
off Parklands Road
Westlands, PO Box 12349
Sarit Centre, Nairobi, **Kenya**
Tel: (+254)- 2 - 3743 572
Fax: (+254) - 2 - 3743 885

Cocoteros 172
Col. Nueva Santa Maria
Mexico City DF 02800, **Mexico**
Tel: (+52) - 5 - 556 2152
Fax: (+52) - 5 - 556 2468
✉ ombkmex@infosel.net.mx